The Pack Sweeps on Together

Dedicated to Pat Calnan

Special mention to:
Bill Clapham, Chris Haines
and Steve and Sue Cluney

Published by New Generation Publishing in 2024

Text © John E Turner and Blackheath & Bromley Harriers AC

First Edition

The author asserts the moral right under the Copyright, Designs and Patents Act 1988 to be identified as the author of this work. British Library Cataloguing in Publication Data.

A catalogue record for this book is available from the British Library.
ISBN: 978-1-83563-141-6

All Rights reserved. No part of this publication may be reproduced, stored in a retrieval system or transmitted, in any form or by any means without the prior consent of the author, nor be otherwise circulated in any form of binding or cover other than that which it is published and without a similar condition being imposed on the subsequent purchaser.
www.newgeneration-publishing.com

Front cover design and book layout by Peter Rogers

The Pack Sweeps on Together

The Blackheath Harriers' Gazette

1979-2000

Extracts selected by John E Turner

The Lay of the Last Harrier

The way was long, the wind was cold,
The harrier was infirm and old.
His tattered shorts and jersey grey,
Seemed to have known a better day.
The last of all the Heathens he
Was plodding on in misery,
For welladay, the rest had fled,
His faster friends were home - in bed
And he, neglected and oppressed,
Wished he were with them and at rest.
No more he pranced with eager bound
Or pattered lightly o'er the ground;
No more at captain's firm request
In every match a welcome guest,
He elbowed others from his way
And took the lead in every fray.
Old times were changed, old manners gone
Now Juniors led the club team home.
The zealots of the coaches' class
Called his efforts just a farce.
A wandering runner, tired and sore,
He stumbled on with feet unsure
And strained to contact at the rear
The race he once had led full clear.

Tom Richards had left him long ago
With Laurie Weatherill well in tow
And Keepax and Reed just close behind
With Hogg and Thomas in conflict twined
Oh that Murray or Aldridge still did race
Or Pirie or Pollard to save his face.

He passed where Blackness's muddy track
Leads to Layhams by fierce switchback
Up from Furze Bottom in mud and chalk
He wished he dared but stop and walk.
But on leaden legs he stumbled still
With lungs near bursting, up the hill;
As, light in head, he gained the brow
A linnet sang on a blackened bough.
The watchers who had chanced to wait
To see each runner reach the gate
Muttered perfunctory words of praise
Then hurried back in cars to Hayes.

Across flat fields and down he toiled
Then up again through barbed wire coiled;
A ghastly sight there met him now -
Acre on acre of stubbly plough!
But what was that just in his sight
It couldn't be a trick of light?
His eyes did not deceive him quite
It was a runner - dressed in white!
How strong on man the urge of Hope
Makes failing forces strangely cope
With obstacles that just before
Had seemed to daunt for evermore.
So was it now: his pace did quicken
As shades of night began to thicken.
Over fields and muddy track
The hunt was on; no holding back;
The distance in between the two
Got shorter as they homewards drew.
A hundred yards - he was getting near
The man in front looked round in fear.
Now he too knows a race is on

They struggle each, all caution gone.
Oblivious, they forget the Fox
Until it takes its toll and knocks
Them both aback with eyes a-pop
To start again once at the top
As the breath comes back again
It's but twenty yards between the men.
For half a mile they struggle, then
The twenty yards reduced to ten,
And when at last the road they reach
They're neck and neck extended each.
There but remains the dreadful path
Where a quarter of a mile seems a mile
and a half.
And neck and neck they gasp and grin.
The other runners cheer them in.
The judges by the finishing booth
Start in fright at the sight uncouth
As the man in black and the man in white
Pass as the passing of day into night:
No space between they come so fast
The judges give them "Equal last."

And did they after suffer pain?
Perhaps they did, but they'd count it gain
For in that pleasant aftermath
When reclining in the bath,
The thought of having done it all
Makes all the other things seem small
And may it ever be that way
For that is why we've raced today.

*Unfortunately, on the copy I have seen,
there is no name and no date.*

Foreword

Let us remember our history and go always forward with pride.

John E Turner

Please note

The month and year, in capitals, shows in which Gazette the item can be found.

The dates, in lower case, show when the events occurred.

Text in italics is my editorial comment.

OCTOBER 1979/MARCH 1980

Track Captain's Message

....On an individual basis 1980 is a very important year for our internationals and everyone in the Club must give them maximum help in order that they can reach their targets of selection for the Olympic Games. It is 1964 since Blackheath last had a representative at these Games, and 1980 presents us with our best chance since that date. Tim Foulger has already achieved the qualifying standard in the high jump, Mike Winch is just a few centimetres away from the shot standard, and our other internationals Trevor Llewelyn, Nick Brooks and Julian Spooner also have a chance.

OCTOBER 1979/MARCH 1980

19th October 1979

Maryon-Wilson Swimming Championship.

....the swimmers were seeded in three heats of four, with the known fastest swimmers in one heat, the known slowest in another and the new faces scattered about. This technique is based on years of study, muscle definition, badges on costumes, shaven legs and the odd question or two regarding holidays at the sea. One face did slip through this tough scrutiny: a cagey old so-and-so and a past president at that! Alan Brent had been training regularly for months prior to the event. After years of swimming to a second either way he knocked 13 seconds off to record a time that he last swam in 1963. (Through gritted teeth - "Well done Alan", - handicapper.)

OCTOBER 1979/MARCH 1980

3rd November 1979

Reigate Priory Cross Country Relay. (6 x 2½ miles)

....Peter Hannell brought the 'B' team home in 22nd place. He was racing the Salisbury '15' the next day and so only really went to watch at Reigate!

The 'A' team finished third, which it is believed the Club has not achieved before. It was just reward for the hard working team-members who were really very concerned that the wait for the prize presentation would cause them to miss the fireworks at Hayes later in the evening.

OCTOBER 1979/MARCH 1980

2nd December 1979

Rowing Match v Ranelagh Harriers.

The "Frankeiss Cup" has been fought for annually since it was presented just fifty years ago. We were the holders as a result of a hotly contested event last year. Our team started all right but was soon in trouble. Apparently there was a disparity in pulling weights. This had the effect of our boat showing a strong inclination to turn to starboard (right to you landlubbers). In fact there was at one time a likelihood of our craft running ashore and finishing up in the local High Street! This tendency did not help our chances one little bit and in spite of helpful comments and/or abuse from supporters on the towpath we finished second.

JULY/OCTOBER 1980

Editorial.

....If all goes to plan, there should be some field events facilities at Norman Park by the time you receive this Gazette. It is certainly a dream come true for Blackheath that a track has been installed so close to Bourne Way - and an all-weather track at that!

Bromley Council must be persuaded that it is for everybody's sake that lighting and a full range of facilities is made available in the very near future. A sure way to help them on their way is to use the track. It is open throughout daylight hours, so even if you can't make it during the week, a Sunday morning session must surely be possible for most?

Norman Park's track is the most valuable property in the area for Blackheath - USE IT!

JULY/OCTOBER 1980

11th October 1980
Hon. Secretary's Report.

"Mr President, gentlemen.

I have pleasure in presenting the 111th Annual Report of Blackheath Harriers for the year ending August 31st 1980.

Membership at that date was 690, consisting of 160 life members, 330 seniors and 200 juniors. During the year there were 44 deletions and 25 resignations. 111 new members were elected."

...."Individually, 1980 was a disappointing season with all our Olympics hopefuls being unsuccessful in their ambitions of going to Moscow. Mike Winch continued the season as Britain's number two shot putter and, with the retirement of Geoff Capes, takes over as number one."

JULY/OCTOBER 1980

Milk & Sport.

The long-awaited sponsorship deal between Blackheath Harriers and Express Dairies Co. Ltd. has at last materialised - much to the delight of ourselves and the Kent A.A.A.!

Grateful thanks are due to Express Dairies for their generosity on November 8th when they supplied so many goodies for the Kent Boys, Colts and Vet's Cross-Country Championships at Sparrows Den. Apart from one minor hitch when the milk float became stuck in the mud, all went well.

NOVEMBER 1980/MARCH 1981

The First London Marathon. 1981.

Chris Haines reports....

Nothing had happened quite like this through the streets of London ever before. The media, with their pre-race ballyhoo and the enthusiasm of Chris Brasher, swamped the organisers with over 7,000 entries. The lead into the race began last November with preliminary announcements, and the sending out of entry forms early this year. The Club offered help at an early stage, but not until the last minute were we asked to help in the processing of entries.

The large number of entries from the Club was evident from the renewed interest in pack running from the Club HQ on Wednesday nights, and by a Tatsfield splinter group on Sunday mornings. The usual preparations were carried out: long slow runs played havoc with the Cross-Country Captain's selection policy for both the 'Southern' and the 'National'!

The three days prior to the race were set aside for the collection of numbers and a bag - sadly deficient of goodies - from the Strand Palace Hotel. Here again, several Blackheathens were in evidence assisting with the administration, welcoming runners with such phrases as "Have a sweat band" (Gordon Brooks) or "Hello, ugly" (Gordon Hickey). No amount of praise could bring forth the promised T-shirts, said to be covered by the entry fee, though!

After an extra-early night (the clocks went forward that evening), it was still decidedly unpleasant trying to wake up and have breakfast in time for the race - between 5 and 6 a.m.! But with however many scientific aids at his disposal, each athlete is still a law unto himself as regards the final meals before the race. The variations, sworn to have unbelievable effects, ranged from toast and cereal, through to a good fried breakfast - or nothing at all! Whatever was eaten though, the adrenalin soon played its part with most members arriving in Greenwich Park in good time.

It was especially pleasing to be assisted by so many club officials in checking in, finding the relevant buses for tracksuits to be taken to the finish, and being pointed in the right direction for the legendary 100-foot urinal!

The race got under way at 9 a.m. sharp and from the outset the noise of the helicopters above, and the crowd on the route, was deafening. Even among the million or so spectators one could identify a friendly face here and there. There was so much support for everyone that you couldn't help but run and run and run.

The last few hundred yards past the Palace to Constitution Hill will always be remembered by everyone, together with the superb services at the finish, but would we ever reach the giant digital clock on the horizon? Brief words were exchanged with other runners when we happened to meet, and then - the long trek home.

What had been missed by those who had participated was shown at 4 p.m. that afternoon. The superb pictures produced by the BBC TV coverage showed the absolute measure of the event. Of course those who had run simply wished to see themselves, but what was evident to me was the pleasure that running had given to so many athletes, spectators and joggers. It was wonderful to see youngsters respond to the challenge of veterans and ladies in the race. Everyone helped each other.

Club result:

132nd	Chris Haines	2.29.41
135th	Peter Shepheard	2.29.47
138th	Graham Martin	2.29.54

Only these three managed to beat Joyce Smith (2.29.56) the winner of the women's title.

Another personal best by John Baldwin (2.33.58) only moved him down from 15th to 17th on the Blackheath Harriers' 'all-time' list.

The Club had just under 50 finishers.

SEPTEMBER/NOVEMBER 1981

Hon. Secretary's Report.

....we have had the Club rewired at a cost of about £2,000 so please be as generous as you can with a donation.

....Mrs. Daniels, our cook, still manages to provide us with excellent meals at a very reasonable cost. We are all "internally" grateful to both Mrs. Daniels and those who serve us on the Wine Committee. Peter Hannell, Chris Haines and Gordon Hickey must put in a lot of time on our behalf.

SEPTEMBER/NOVEMBER 1981

The A.G.M. seen from the back row. (Extracts)

On the evening of the 17th October, 1981, another stitch was sewn into life's rich tapestry; I attended (who?) my first Annual General Meeting of the Harriers. From previous experience in cycling and climbing circles I knew that these affairs could span a wide spectrum of diversion from the electrifyingly riveting to something akin to watching grey paint dry in a chapel in Blaenau Ffestiniog on a November Wednesday afternoon. It can be safely said, though, that the Harriers 112th AGM approached neither extreme.

If I suspected at the outset that I had let myself in for a marathon for which I was not properly trained, I was convinced by the time the Hon. Minutes Secretary had monologued the report of last year's meeting. Surely it was an eternal optimist who named such reports 'minutes'!

....Next onto his feet was a gangling fidgeting youth representing the Wine Committee who wittered on about dwindling profits, pint glasses and the price of mince. However, I don't recall too much of this as I was thankfully distracted by a small fly on the floor with a damaged wing which seemed doomed to spend the rest of its life rotating on its axis. By the time the poor creature had expired we were reaching the stage when the new President was to be announced. The air buzzed with apathy. It turned out to be Ian. C. Wilson which was clearly not universally expected judging by the number of quids that immediately started to change hands.

There was a rendition of the Club cry by Laurie Hammill, hanky waving, false teeth clackerlacking.

What remained of the evening was spent aimlessly wandering about consuming and spilling shepherd's pie and booze. In other words, life returned pretty much to normal.

SEPTEMBER/NOVEMBER 1981

Advert

Get your Club kit from Centresport at the National Sports Centre, Crystal Palace. (Open 7 days a week).

Club kitbag - £7.95

Vests. From XS at £3.50 to XL at £5.50

Shorts. New design (available early 1982) £4.50. And with inner brief £5.50.

Weather suits. Specially made in Club Colours by Karhu of Finland. Wind-proof and waterproof, both jacket and trousers fully lined. Suit - £27. Jacket - £15.50. Trousers - £12.50.

Sweatshirts. Top quality American. Children's - £5.25 and adults - £6.25.

T-shirts. 100% cotton. Children's - £2.25 and adults - £2.75.

Ask for Graham Botley or Ken Daniel.

DECEMBER 1981/JUNE 1982

Postscript to Punchbowl Night.

A certain Past-President who did not imbibe too much punch at the festivities, but did get involved in mixing it, arranged for his chauffeuse to collect him at midnight. She duly arrived and after the usual 30 minute delay, managed to get him into the car and away home. On reaching home, she remarked on his inability to string together two coherent punch lines to tell a joke, and suggested he try his mechanical ability by opening the garage door.

He climbed from the car and swung the up and over door in motion. As it slowly arced upwards the car headlights lit the garage interior like a stage. Bearing in mind the musical tone of the evening the Past-President swung round and went into a song and dance routine.

Unfortunately, at this juncture, the garage door reached the end of its travel, hit the rubber stop, and bounced back on the return journey, accelerating en route. It came down on the head of the Past President with a resounding clang - whereupon he went into his funny walks routine.

At this moment in time he felt no pain but awoke in the morning with an egg sized lump, surmounted by a cut and his hair matted with dried blood. His chauffeuse thought the grimace of pain was due to a well-earned hangover, but burst into hysterical laughter when shown the injury.

The moral of this tale is - beware if you aspire to be a star - you might end up seeing them.

DECEMBER 1981/JUNE 1982

The New 200 Group.

The new 200 Group eventually got off the ground in September, 1981, the subscription level having been raised to £2 per month and the prize list adjusted accordingly. Currently there are 128 members participating in this unique experiment in the redistribution of wealth (Haines style), the only certainty being that large four-figure sums will be raised for the benefit of the Club. Vacancies still exist and if you are not a member, feel lonely, and that you are missing something - you are!

DECEMBER 1981/JUNE 1982

2nd April 1982
The Blackheath Harriers Marathon Clinic. At Hayes.

In view of the marathon running epidemic and in particular with the London Marathon only just round the corner in every sense of the phrase, it was decided that the Club should open its doors to those local people infected with the disease. The evening of the 2nd April was chosen and an encouraging 50-plus aspirants duly trooped in and sat themselves down. To a person they appeared to be full of miles in anticipation and it fell to the panel of Alan Brent (chairman), Dave Chettle (best of 2 hours and 10 minutes), Don Faircloth (1970 Commonwealth Silver Medal), Bob Richardson (Club record Holder with 2 hours and 17 minutes), Chris Haines, Ian Wilson and Graham Martin, the organiser, to reassure, instruct, advise and warn from their own not inconsiderable experiences of racing in general and of the 26.2 miles in particular.

If the audience expected a blueprint to instant success then they were going to be disappointed:

a) because they were soon made to realise that there were virtually as many approaches as there were runners, and

b) because Chris Haines had made up his mind that his principal role that evening was to disagree with virtually everything everybody else said.

Whilst this might well have guaranteed that any confidence the novices may have had when they arrived was well and truly stripped away by the time they left, it did at the same time ensure a very entertaining evening. There were, of course, a number of incontrovertible do's and don'ts regarding pace, liquid intake and clothing which were strongly emphasised.

By and large therefore everyone felt the exercise, which had been admirably orchestrated by Graham Martin, had been well worthwhile, and would possibly be the embryo of bigger things to come of this nature.

JULY/OCTOBER 1982

From the President's Closing Message for 1981/82.

....Cross-Country events will be reduced to chaos unless the trail layers (most of whom are over 70!) get help from younger members.

Nothing much changes! (2023.)

JULY/OCTOBER 1982

Hon. Secretary's Report. 1982.

....Since the amendment of Club Rules two years ago Life Membership has no longer been obtainable by purchase, but may be awarded by the committee on the recommendation of the President, Hon. Secretary or Hon. Treasurer.

JULY/OCTOBER 1982

17th July 1982.
Southern League Division 2. Hornchurch.

Result.
5,000m, John Baldwin - 14m 57.0s (U.K. over 45 age best).

JULY/OCTOBER 1982

The Old Poly and New Trophy.

With the sad death of A.G.V. Allen recently and the inception of a trophy for the Club Marathon Championship in his honour this year, it seemed appropriate to publish the extract below penned by A.G.V. Allen concerning his experience in the 1932 Poly Marathon and published that year in the Gazette.

JULY/OCTOBER 1982

Saturday 28th May 1932.
The Story of the Polytechnic Marathon.

I had the morning off from the office, in view of the Marathon so I did not get up until 8.30 in consequence of which, by the time I had had breakfast, done a lot of odd jobs and packed my bag it was nearly time for lunch.

At 11 o'clock I had a large steak and potatoes and afterwards caught the 11.37 to Charing Cross where I waited, under Hungerford Bridge, for Mobbs and Holmes to arrive. Mobbs appeared first but Holmes came along shortly afterwards. We then went in search of the Green Line bus for Windsor but it had not arrived at the terminus. It was due to leave at 12.30 but did not arrive until after that, setting off again about 12.40. It was not a good journey down as having taken nearly an hour over the first five miles we all had wind up about not arriving in time. However, once on the Great West Road the driver made up for lost time and we arrived in Windsor only 20 minutes late at 2.05. Alighting we made our way to the Great Western Railway Station and first of all saw the doctor, who examined heart and lungs with great thoroughness. After this we changed in one of the waiting rooms allotted specially for the purpose, taking special care over greasing and shoe-tying, etc.

We were called out for the start at about 10 minutes to 3 and we marched up from the station to the Windsor Castle drive, where having lined up for the start, we were given a few rather unnecessary instructions and then we all stood by until the exact stroke of 3 o'clock when we were sent off by L.F. (Jimmy) Tremeer who used the pistol which started the original Windsor to London Marathon in 1908.

Holmes went ahead of us straight away as he had made out a faster schedule than we were attempting. Mobbs and I were only out to try for

Standard Award (that is to cover the course inside 3 hours 15 minutes) so we intended running together throughout which we did and which proved to be a great help to both of us. So we started quite slowly going about the same pace that we used in training for a couple of miles into Slough, then gradually increasing pace. We set out to do the first 10 miles in 67½ minutes. For a long time Holmes was in sight about 300 yards ahead - we were about 25th position or lower but he disappeared after a while. At about 5 miles we were informed as to the time we had taken by Wilkinson and McIvor of Blackheath Harriers who were traversing the course in a car mainly for that purpose.

There were huge crowds of people out to see the race at various points en route but there was a pretty good sprinkling in even the most isolated spots on the course and what struck me was the percentage who had programmes. There must have been a huge sale. Funnily enough, too, some of the people who saw our numbers as we approached, apparently consulted the programme to see who we were for we were greeted by several complete strangers with shouts of "Good old Mobbs" or "Well run, Allen, up Blackheath!"

We passed the 10 miles mark in 65¼ minutes, much faster going than we intended but as we were both running as easily as possible we did not worry. We were informed that Holmes was about two minutes ahead, he having done the first 10 in about 63½ minutes. I expected the 7 mile stretch of main London road from Uxbridge to be tedious but we did not notice it at all. We both ran without any trouble at all though I had fears of Mobbs getting cramp at one time which fortunately did not materialise.

Just before we turned off the main road we caught up with Holmes! He was running very easily so we suggested that it was time to let himself go and he forged ahead gradually after running with us for a quarter of a mile. We covered 20 miles in about 2 hours 12 minutes. Excellent going in view of our proposed schedule of about 2 hours 20 minutes. I had fears that we were going too fast to last but we both seemed untroubled, having conversed gaily all the way.

Two or three times during the race we were offered sponges soaked in water and Eau de Cologne to wipe our faces. These were very refreshing.

We were still running very strongly at Kew Bridge and I personally only began to tire at all about the 23rd mile. We must both have been very fit and thoroughly trained. As we neared the end of our journey the roadside crowds grew more and more encouraging in their very enthusiastic applause, and when after the last stretch of road we arrived at the Stamford Bridge ground and still running side by side emerged on to the track for the two laps to complete the race, we were greeted with tremendous applause. The track was in an appalling condition after the afternoon's events there and very soggy but we plodded round, still running very well I think and, linking arms, ran in together in 2 hours 58 minutes 38 seconds.

I felt quite fresh though glad it was the end. I learnt that Holmes had got up as far as 11th. We tied for 14th place Mobbs and I, which I was very bucked about.

It had been a really great day and the most pleasing thing about the result was that by our combined efforts we put Blackheath in 3rd place for team honours.

Result:

1st S. Ferris (RAF) 2h 36m 32s.

2nd T. Lalande (Herne Hill) 2h 43m 30s.

3rd J. Slaney 2h 44m 6s.

11th W. Holmes 2h 54m 9s.

NOVEMBER 1982/APRIL 1983

A Computer War!

Trevor Walhen, British Decathlete, Blackheath Harrier, Chief Petty Officer in the Royal Navy, and computer enthusiast, was made an Honorary member of the Sinclair Computers Users Club in 1982, in recognition of his part in the Falklands conflict.

Trevor is an electronics engineer aboard HMS Hermes and took his Sinclair ZX81 to the Falklands in case he should have some spare time. Despite working 8 p.m. to 8 a.m. he usually found a couple of hours for his Sinclair when he came off duty. During this time he designed a game which he aptly entitled "HMS Hermes" and then sent it to the Sinclair Users Magazine. It features his own ship against Argentinian Super Etendard aircraft armed with deadly Exocet missiles and an enemy submarine.

MAY/OCTOBER 1983

Limited offer - Apply Now.

A recent reappraisal of the present situation revealed that a few vacancies exist for keen club members whose chances of winning anything from the Winter Handicapper are now non-existent.

Applicants should possess a weatherproof physique and good sight. A sense of humour is essential. Map reading and first aid techniques would be advantageous. A crash course on flag laying (devised from the ancient Indian art of pig-sticking) will be available on request.

The twin virtues of stamina and stoicism will be required, also cheerfulness in adverse conditions. If you feel you can meet these challenging demands, contact the Chief Trail Layer, Journeys End, 56, Bourne Way, Hayes, Kent.

MAY/OCTOBER 1983

Gazette printed by F.A.Slugg & Co.Ltd. Trowbridge, Wiltshire.

(Me - sorry - I just like strange names)

NOVEMBER 1983/APRIL 1984

4th December 1983.
The "Boat Race". At Kew

(Pure coincidence - but I am writing this on Sunday 3rd April 2022 - and under an hour ago was "The Boat Race". This report however was of the annual row against Ranelagh Harriers.)

Any sportsman of whatever persuasion will tell you that the secret of success is painstaking preparation - a meticulous attention to detail that ensures that cometh the crucial hour the mind and body are perfectly tuned to concert pitch and harmonised to a degree of precision that transcends the world of physical effort and moves into an arena of pure art.

Thus it was not, in the case of the Heathen rowing squad. By the time they found themselves bobbing and weaving all skewiff at the start line, the crew had amassed a total experience of 3 outings on the river and not all of those together. The balance of the four rowers was immediately suspect. Bob Cliff skilled from his college days but not the sort of powerhouse one looks for in a rower, was, like Keith Coombs, reliable and steady but Daryl Brand's bulk meant he should have rowed alone on one side with the other three oars on the other, so powerful was his pulling. The fourth man in the engine room was Chris Reynolds, who had never rowed before in his life. Les Roberts, the cox, was also completely new to the water, which he eventually admitted even extended to not being able to swim; wonderfully reassuring stuff when you are mid-stream with speeding launches and lumbering barges every which way.

Believe it or not, despite everything, our outfit almost showed some semblance of form once or twice but not enough to prevent them getting well and truly stuffed by the relatively slick Ranelagh lads. Still, much was learned by our greenhorns; we will not be so conclusively walloped next year.

NOVEMBER 1983/APRIL 1984

Mob Matches - A Beginner's Guide.

What are they? A question I certainly asked myself when I tried to fathom the intricacies of my first winter fixture card. Unfortunately, being lazy by nature it was a question that was left unanswered for far too long on my part. Upon enlightenment I realised that I'd only just avoided being lynched for my non-participation in previous years. Pure ignorance of the unwritten rule (many argue that the obvious need not be stated) that all members must run in these matches to call themselves true "Heathens", seemed to be no excuse.

Well, go on and explain, you say. Here goes. They consist of three matches versus South London Harriers, Orion Harriers and Ranelagh Harriers, which are on an alternate home and away basis. They are run over the country and the key point is that virtually everyone scores. When was the last time you scored in the 'A' team?

The scoring system is simple. Each side scores 3 less than the number of starters of the smaller side, so nearly everyone scores and having numerical advantage is vital for success. Above all, the matches are a real test of Club as distinct from individual strength.

Why should you in particular run? Principally because they are arranged for all 'Heathens, and obviously Club success is vital for the morale of any club. However, I would argue that there are even stronger reasons for running.

Blackheath is the oldest combined cross-country and athletic club in the United Kingdom, or for that matter the whole civilised world and is a club that is proud of its traditions despite these being "unfashionable" today. The strong sense of identity and continuity all 'Heathens feel stems from events like these and the pride all of us feel in being part of such a well known club, both inside and outside athletics, is a result of this. We all live off its reputation which in turn enhances our own status, something that a member of, say, Shin-splint Joggers could never have. These traditions can only be maintained by us now and surely there is a greater sense of occasion about the Nicholls Cup race, a race of nearly 90 years standing, than say the "Inaugural Allhallows 5".

A resurgence of interest came about early this year with 87 'Heathens turning out against Ranelagh away from home. But to beat South London Harriers (to whom we have lost for the last six years, often narrowly) we need more runners! The dates versus South London and Ranelagh (mid November and January respectively) should be fixed points in everyone's racing calendar as they are fixtures in which members can repay to the Club many of the advantages it offers to them.

"Am I good enough?" you may ask. I certainly felt that my contributions would be of little use until I first ran and discovered the immense range of ability in Mob Matches.

A 65 minute 10 miler will normally finish in the top half of the field. If only 10 or 15 more members of such a standard turned out each time then they would walk away happy men, content in the knowledge that their contributions had tipped the balance towards us regaining the cups.

Every year some of our finest past runners (some ex-internationals) re-emerge from retirement to run in these fixtures, such is the importance.

So come on you "New" Harriers who have yet to discover the pleasure of the run, the bath, the bread, butter and jam, and the pot of tea. Do support these races. Who knows, you might yet discover that you enjoy both the terrain and above all the friendship that cross-country racing is known for. K.P.

MAY/NOVEMBER 1984

In the Editorial....

Thanks to the sterling, stirring efforts and innovation of our new winter captain Graham Botley, the word was spread far and wide and the response was tremendous; a new Mob Match turn out record of 130 'Heathens.

....Moving away from the athletic side there is also a growing feeling up on the bridge that there is a need for some repair elsewhere to the Club's fabric. In short, the disquiet is about a lack of dignity that is becoming ever more evident at our functions. Failure to respond to the President's gavel and similar calls to order is a case in point although to my mind this is not so much a loss of dignity as simply an absence of common courtesy, and may even be evidence of a lack of real interest. We also seem to have largely forgotten that members' families and friends and representatives of other clubs are our guests when attending club functions and should be treated as such and not left to fend for themselves.

MAY/NOVEMBER 1984

The First Olympics - Athens 1896.

Coming to your T.V. screens at some stage in the form of one of those mini series you love to hate is America's answer to "Chariots of Fire", "The First Olympics - Athens 1896." If the NBC are going to win any awards it certainly won't be for the originality of the title.

"The First Olympics" tells the story of the American team's preparation for the Games, and follows its journey across the Atlantic arriving in Athens only just in time for the opening ceremony on 6th April. The Americans had planned to arrive with plenty of time in hand but Greece was still using the Julian calendar, so the 6th April became 25th March and they were lucky not to miss the Games altogether.

Britain fielded only four athletes of whom one was convalescing in Athens following an illness, and another was in Greece primarily to compete in the weight-lifting. One reason advanced for our absence was that Oxford and Cambridge Universities (who virtually made up the British team in those days) refused to answer the letter of invitation because it was in French.

The film, made for NBC Television by Columbia Pictures, is a five hour epic (?) to be screened over two nights when the BBC or ITV get round to it.

Your friendly neighbourhood assistant editor (T. Llewelyn) was fortunate enough (fortunate if you like spending 2 weeks in Athens in November getting up at the crack of dawn and waiting around in a Greek stadium, with little or no cover, for the rain to stop so that you can triple jump in shorts that come down to your knees, on a surface resembling porridge, into wet sand!) to bear a reasonable resemblance to the very good looking American actor David Caruso (last seen nearly drowning in "An Officer and a Gentleman") who plays James Connolly, an Irish American who, in winning the triple jump (with 13.71m, 44' 11") became the first ever Modern Olympic champion.

The company spent a small fortune having my hair dyed orange so that I could double for Caruso in the jumping sequences. He had injured his knee playing American football and could barely jog let alone triple jump.

MAY/NOVEMBER 1984

20th October 1984
Hon. Secretary's Report.

....At the end of September membership of the Club stood at 928, including 140 Life Members. During the year 7 deaths were reported and there were 31 resignations, making a total of 38 losses compared with 177 elections. Certainly the highest totals in the Club's history.

MAY/NOVEMBER 1984

News from far and near.
September

Congratulations and donation from Archie Peachey for the Gazette - another accolade for the indefatigable editor. (Les Roberts). The addition of a number to his (Peachey's) house will ensure prompt deliveries in future. He noticed a reference to a woman competitor as "also a member of the South London Harriers!!!! Don't tell me - I'm sure we wouldn't !!!??" He has been assured and sleeps soundly now.

Also.

Cecil Harden from Rochester remembers E.J.J. Reed and Dick Cockburn running on Charlton Park Track. He has a distinct recollection of passing Sydney Wooderson in a Hayes race. (When somebody had trodden on the heel of Sydney's shoe and he had stopped to put it on again!)

October

Clifford Davies of Yeoville, South Africa, was visited by Harold Thompson (Past President) and duly presented with his 50 year mug. (A worldwide service.)

MAY/NOVEMBER 1984

Obituaries.

Elizabeth Daniels - "Mrs. D."

It is with much sadness that we record the passing of Mrs. Daniels. Mrs. D. came to the Club some twenty years ago when her son and daughter-in-law were our resident stewards. At that time twenty people sitting down to supper was considered a crowd, but such was Mrs. Daniels' reputation for good, plain cooking, that numbers gradually escalated to the one hundred plus that she cooked for at Christmas Suppers.

MAY/NOVEMBER 1984

Club Marathon Championship. (London Marathon) Blackheath to Westminster. May 1984.

In all we had 114 finishers on the day, and first home for the second successive year was Richard Coles in 2.26.19.

MAY/NOVEMBER 1984

17th November 1984

78th Mob Match v South London Harriers. At Coulsdon.

This day saw the emergence of a new enthusiasm in cross-country running in Blackheath Harriers. Not only did all the established faces turn out but also a very high percentage of the new blood attached to the Club over the last year or so. I hope they enjoyed it and that the momentum will be sustained. A new Club record of 130 Heathens started the race which we won by dint of the sheer weight of numbers.

Keep it up lads, this is what it's all about.

DECEMBER 1984/SEPTEMBER 1985

Things they say:-

"Where have all the others gone?" Les Roberts to Bill O'Donnell towards the end of a 10 mile training run covered at only just outside 5 minute mile pace.

"The trouble with vets' races is finding your tracksuit afterwards in a sack full of toupées, false teeth and hearing aids." Brian Buonvino, Dartford Harriers.

"Mum, I'm phoning to tell you I've won the European Championship." Reply: (pause) "Oh, that's good; when did you find out?"

"Mum, I'm just phoning to tell you I've won the World Championship." Reply: "Oh, I am pleased" (pause) "My foot has really been giving me gip this week."

DECEMBER 1984/SEPTEMBER 1985

Letters to the Editor. December 1984.

Dear Sir,

It has been grand in recent years to see such a famous old club as ours maintaining its traditions and successfully evolving with the times. Our record in the National Athletic League speaks for itself, as does the redevelopment of the club house.

There is, however, one major area in which we are sadly lagging behind. Women's athletics has really taken off, and many clubs have a thriving women's section. The fact that we do not in 1984 is an anachronism. There are a number of families involved with Blackheath Harriers, and it is regrettable that not all their active athletes can be club members.

Would not Blackheath and Bromley A.C. be a fine name for a rejuvenated club ready to go on to even greater success over a broader field? It would also help to dispel the illusions of prospective new members about the Club's precise location.

Yours 'Heathenly,

Geoff Crowder.

Letters to the Editor. (Continued)

Our late Vice President, A.G.V. Allen, was in the habit of writing notes about races and giving relevant details, and the following extract will surprise those who are not used to pre-war hospitality. He writes about our visit to Cambridge University in 1925: -

"We were escorted to the Livingstone

Hotel where we had a ripping dinner. Tomato soup, filleted plaice and anchovy sauce. Roast goose, peas and potatoes, fruit salad or apple tart with custard, cheese and coffee. The wines were Chablis and Burgundy."

Indeed those were the days!

DECEMBER 1984/SEPTEMBER 1985

Club Marathon Championships. (London Marathon) 21st April 1985. Blackheath to Westminster.

David White	2.38.11.
Barry O'Gorman	2.39.27.
Peter Shepheard	2.40.26.
Stan Ridgewell	2.52.34.
Mike Peel	2.53.59.
John. E. Turner	2.58.27.
Peter Hannell	3.01.36.
Ray Walsh	3.04.01.
Mark Ellison	3.07.08.
John Taylor	3.15.55.
Dave Appleton	3.20.09.
David Carton	3.26.07.

DECEMBER 1984/SEPTEMBER 1985

Obituaries.

Norman Dudley. Vice President.

....For the two seasons 1959/61 he served as Hon. Secretary for the Club and worked unstintingly for it despite the difficulties of having to travel to remote corners of the world in the course of his work as a mining engineer. The influence of this profession was seen in his hobby of producing profile maps of the Club courses showing the heights reached and the steepness of notorious inclines. But the most noteworthy example of this skill was to be found in his organisation of the Centenary Commemorative Run from Peckham to Blackheath to Ladywell to West Wickham and finally to Hayes for which he devised three separate courses for each stage to permit fast, medium and slow packs to rendezvous at the same time. The accompanying maps represented a cartographical triumph.

Obituaries.

T.J.G. Haynes.

We were sorry to hear of the death early in August of T. J. G. Haynes, who joined in the "Green Man" days at Blackheath in October 1920.

His latest communication was gently to query how the Gazette managed to acknowledge a donation from him and in the same issue put him down as a "lost address". But to show no ill feeling he sent another donation! A Novices Pewter from 1920 proudly shared a place on his mantlepiece with his 50 years' membership pot.

SEPTEMBER 1985/APRIL 1986

Editorial.

....Relationships with Bromley Council remain excellent and there is now a firm commitment to build a stand and changing facilities at Norman Park.

....The most gratifying news of late was learning that this here chronicle of Heathen activity had been judged in the top 3 in the nation by Running Magazine. Bearing in mind that one of their chief criteria for a good club news letter was that it had to be up to date and therefore issued frequently, we really shouldn't have stood a chance but, despite this shortcoming, they obviously liked it very much in other ways and so the Club is now richer to the tune of £50 worth of books.

SEPTEMBER 1985/APRIL 1986

Situation Vacant.

Are you interested in ensuring that only three runners beat you in six cross-country races during the 1986/87 season?

If so and you are:

Adept
Analytical
Aware
Enumerate
Impartial
Interested in psychology
Legible
Sceptical
Statistical and
Thick-skinned....

It would also help if you can name/ know about 50% of the starters and have access to a computer.

For further details of this exciting position, please apply to the Hon. Winter Handicapper.

SEPTEMBER 1985/APRIL 1986

19th October 1985.
Hon. Secretary's Report.

At the end of September membership of the Club stood at 994 and at the General Committee meeting there was a net addition of 12 to that number, bringing our "book" total above the 1,000 mark for the first time.

....Much of the credit for our clean sweep in the Mob Matches must go to our new broom, Vice President Gary or Graham Botley, whose enthusiasm and encouragement persuaded many of our newer members to sample the delights of the country for the first time, to the extent that we had 130 starters against South London Harriers, a record number for this fixture, 85 against Orion and Thames Hare and Hounds and 111 against Ranelagh.

....Our warmest congratulations go to Les Roberts on winning the 5,000 metres in the World Veterans Championships at Rome in June.

SEPTEMBER 1985/APRIL 1986

8th February 1986.
Over the Country.

....On a tough 9-mile course near Brighton for the Southern, our strongest six for many years were in the right place to surprise themselves, numerous club supporters, all other competitors, officials and knowledgeable pressmen alike by lifting the Southern Championship for the first time in the history of the Club! It was of course a very special afternoon, the more so because it was so unexpected and offered so much hope for the future. Bill Foster emerged from several injury-plagued seasons to lead the team with great conviction, while Tim Nash and Jerry Barton contributed stirring performances on their winter débuts for the Club. Bill O'Donnell clearly revelled in his performance and was rewarded three fold - a winners team medal, his best championship placing to date and for the first time ahead of Richard Coles. In last year's race Richard led the Club team home in 43rd place - he could not have imagined that he would 'trail' home here our 5th man in 40th place, and take home a gold medal! Pat Calnan, still not comfortable on the country improved 104 places on last year and was both relieved and delighted to be 6th man home. And the most exciting feature of this new winning team? The average age is only 25!

Just half of this star outfit was available for the 'National', but with the addition of the redoubtable Roberts and a fine performance by 'novice' Richard Coe, Bill Foster inspired a very solid team result for 20th place on the picturesque, wintry Town Moor, Newcastle. This was out of nearly 200 teams.

SEPTEMBER 1985/APRIL 1986

21st April 1986.
Boston Marathon.

Very hilly between 15 and 20 miles. 4500 qualified entrants, 3,900 finishers. De Castella's winning time of 2.07.51 must rank this as the greatest marathon ever run to date bearing in mind the course and the conditions. There was no one within 3½ minutes of him. Ingrid Kristiansen was going for sub 2 hours 20 mins in the ladies race but had to settle for 2.24.55. Les Roberts was also looking for 2.20 but found himself out-sprinted by the Norwegian damsel. He finished in 2.24.59 for 38th place and 3rd master.

De Castella's run was worth about $250,000, Ingrid's about $140,000. Les's haul was just $500 so he will not be retiring from work and buying himself a second home in Boulder, Colorado just yet.

SEPTEMBER 1985/APRIL 1986

Letters to the Editor.

Dear Les,

I recently received the latest issue of the Gazette and was most impressed with its high quality production. Presentation, layout and content are superb - you and your team are to be congratulated.

However, I can't believe that Geoff Crowder really wrote that letter! Is this the Geoff we know and love speaking? Or was he the worse for drink? I love the ladies as much as the next man and agree that a Veronique Marot or a Shirley Strong would tempt any hot-blooded male within a fifty mile radius to join the Club but change our name? Never! The day Blackheath Harriers changes its title is the day I join Colchester A.C. Sorry Geoffrey, you've made a bungle!

Yours 'heathenly

Pete Catley

(Looks like an argument is brewing! - Les Roberts, Editor.)

MAY/SEPTEMBER 1986

Notice Board.

At last we have City Ties. Available at the Clubhouse for just £5. We are going to attempt once again to obtain stripey blazers in Club colours. Last time the interest was substantial but not quite enough to make these high quality garments an economic proposition. We have now obtained further quotations. For details see Brian Stone or anyone on the Wine Committee.

MAY/SEPTEMBER 1986

Hon. Secretary's Report.

....Our membership figure at the end of September 1986 stood at just over 1,000, a similar number to last year. The stable membership number is perhaps indicative that the "boom" which came on the back of the London Marathon is now "bottoming out".

....As many of us know from personal experience the great problem of obtaining success is not encouraging or cajoling the maximum from the team once they are competing but getting them to the starting line at all.

....Any reservations we had hitherto harboured about our own accommodation due to the cess pit have hopefully now disappeared thanks to BHHQ and the initiative of Past President Jim Day, the work of Past President Ian Wilson and Vice President Jack Braughton under the direction of Past President Laurie Hammill which saw us connected to main drainage this year.

MAY/SEPTEMBER 1986

The Dreamer's Mile.
By Mike Cronin

So you have trained
To some degree;
And now before you is the task,
There is no certainty, only a hope;
Alone and waiting,
Moments of hesitation dispelled by a word,
Suddenly, the world is moving,
The dream becomes a reality.

MAY/SEPTEMBER 1986

Young Athletes. 1986.

....How can anyone properly do justice to the efforts of so many young athletes in a season that saw Blackheath Harriers finish as the number two club in the country? The Club's youth programme has finally blossomed into full-blooded success, and let's hope that, with the advent of our new coaching initiative in 1986-7, we can maintain the momentum well into future years.

OCTOBER 1986/APRIL 1987

President's Plea for the Fire Escape.

"Hanging onto a donation could well burn more than a hole in your pocket."

Budget estimate for installation of fire escape - £4,000 to £5,000. Amount received and promised - £2,000.

OCTOBER 1986/APRIL 1987

What are they up to now?

....Johnnie Walker and Don Gillate called on Past President Dick Cockburn at his home near Southwold (Suffolk) at the beginning of May. His best wishes go to all his old friends at Hayes and his 50 year pot, brought up and presented last autumn by Past President Bill Lake, stands in a proud and prominent position to help keep them in mind.

He found it difficult to comprehend that we now had members prepared even to consider changing the sex of the Club, let alone its name. It was beyond his visitors to offer any comforting and reasoned explanation so they all had a good cry. *(Hopefully the "Club Cry".)*

OCTOBER 1986/APRIL 1987

The Way Forward - Questionnaire Results.

1) Should your committee consider admitting ladies to the membership of Blackheath Harriers?

	Yes	No	Don't know	Response Rate
All members	61%	37.5%	1.1%	36.8%
Past Presidents	47.4%	52.6%	-	73.1%
Vice Presidents	50%	47.1%	2.9%	54.8%
Development Sub-committee	75%	25%	-	50%

2) Should your committee explore the possibility of a merger with Bromley Ladies A.C.?

	Yes	No	Don't know
All members	56.2%	43.4%	0.4%
Past Presidents	57.9%	42.1%	-
Vice Presidents	52.9%	44.1%	2.9%
Development Sub-committee	75%	25%	-

3) Should the name Blackheath Harriers remain unaltered?

	Yes	No	Don't know
All members	81.3%	13.6%	5.1%
Past Presidents	84.2%	5.3%	10.5%
Vice Presidents	79.4%	17.7%	2.9%
Development Sub-committee	75%	25%	-

4) Alternative acceptable names:

Blackheath and Bromley A.C.	27.7%
Blackheath and Bromley Harriers	24.2%
Bromley and Blackheath Harriers	7.2%
Bromley and Blackheath A.C.	2.4%
Blackheath and Bromley Ladies A.C.	10.8%
Miscellaneous	27.7%

The general committee has now appointed a sub-committee to investigate the practical implications of these results.

OCTOBER 1986/APRIL 1987

24th January 1987.

South of Thames Senior Cross-Country Championships. Wimbledon Common.

....The team finished 13th out of 30 teams.

This race was first run in 1888 when it was won by W. Jones of Reindeer Harriers.

MAY/SEPTEMBER 1987

Hon. Secretary's Report.

....Although the Ted Pepper 7 attracted a lower entry than previous years Les Roberts did well to finish 2nd with newcomer David Taylor 8th and Pat Calnan 9th giving us 3rd team place. Thanks are due to Simon Parsons for his organisation.

....To mark the 50th anniversary of Sydney Wooderson's world mile record, Gary Spencer conceived the idea of a celebrity mile race. This materialised with a handicap mile included in the I.A.C. Miller Lite meeting at Crystal Palace to which Sydney and a number of his contemporaries were invited as Club guests. In the race the Club was represented by Alan Guilder, Chris McGeorge, Dave Heath and Mike Laws, lined up against the likes of Steve Crabb, Mike Boit and Jack Buckner. The event proved very popular with the crowd, the Press and TV commentators alike.

Phil Davies also showed Club colours on TV when he lined up against World Champion, Ben Johnson, at Crystal Palace in an invitation 100 metres.

....The Club's affairs have continued to be recorded in a most entertaining manner by the Editor of the Gazette, Les Roberts, and his team, but the highlight of the Club's journalistic endeavours is the reappearance of the Courier thanks to the efforts of Bill Clapham.

....Each year the support we receive from the Social Club proves invaluable and this year has seen the gift of a starters PA system for Norman Park, the re-upholstering of chairs, new tablecloths and cutlery together with a commitment of £1,000 towards the new fire escape to match the Club's efforts; a disco was held and we have benefited from the provision of refreshments at Hayes HQ and Norman Park.

....During the course of the year a questionnaire was circulated to all paid up members over the age of 13 resident in the U.K. to ascertain the views on whether further consideration should be given to admitting women to membership, merging with Bromley Ladies A.C. and related to these issues, changing the Club's name. The committee considered the response was sufficient to set up a sub-committee encompassing most points of view to discuss the practical implications of such issues. The sub-committee has met twice and has also held an exploratory meeting with Bromley Ladies to learn their views.

Some members have evinced concern over the mere discussion of such issues. However, the Club has been in existence since 1869 and has survived, whilst others have disappeared off the athletic map, by having the perspicacity to foresee the changes happening in our sport and acting in advance of, rather than responding to them.

OCTOBER 1987/APRIL 1988

The National Cross-Country Championships. Newark. 20th February. 1988.

....Jerry Barton leading the entire field (2,136 finished) around the first turn - a moment captured and the following week a centre-spread photo in Athletics Weekly. It was probably the strongest team yet fielded by the Club, including that of 40 years earlier led by Sydney Wooderson.

Results took a long time to come through, and half our team disappeared back to the hotel, happy with their performances individually and collectively, with talk of a team position comfortably in the top ten. (230 teams closed in). Then when rumour gave way to the confirmed result, the Captain had to make a panic call to the hotel and recall his troops - "get back here boys, you've placed 3rd team!" The presentation was understandably a joyous affair. A few tears were shed, a magnificent trophy for first Southern Team collected and Richard Coles was seen to leap a long way off the floor at confirmation of his medal. What a just reward for his service to the Club, including 13 consecutive appearances in the National.

Blackheath Team

34	Jerry Barton	47.10
41	Bill Foster	47.28
71	Alan Guilder	48.14
83	Tim Nash	48.30
114	Mark Jones	49.11
174	Richard Coles	50.07
262	Mark Colpus	51.01
667	Dave Heath	54.31

1st Team	Birchfield Harriers	248pts
2nd Team	Tipton Harriers	369 pts
3rd Team	Blackheath Harriers	516 pts
4th Team	Invicta/East Kent	540 pts

MAY 1988/MARCH 1989

From the Gazette September to December 1966.

Car parking space in the Club grounds is restricted and the co-operation of members is essential if maximum benefit is to be gained.

Car owners are therefore requested to make use of the rough ground as much as possible, and, those parking in the front rank, to leave a gap for entry to and exit from the rear.

23 years on and nothing has changed. Reassuring or infuriating?

MAY 1988/MARCH 1989

Where are they now?

On two occasions recently, letters were addressed to a life member. As no reply was forthcoming to either of these, a third was duly sent informing the member that if still no acknowledgement was received it would be assumed that he no longer lived at the address shown on the membership list. This elicited the following response: "We have lived at this address for ten years and Mr.... did not live here before then. I have written before this but must add I have enjoyed your magazine immensely and as a pensioner/jogger will miss it. Many thanks. Kath Cotter."

As Kath's original letter does not appear to have been received by the Club, she has been receiving, not only

Gazettes, but fixture lists, notices of A.G.M.s etc. for over 10 years!

Seriously, it does illustrate the importance of letting us know of changes of address, particularly in the case of life members.

Incidentally, it was decided that Kath could continue to receive the Gazette. If the Club ever becomes mixed then she will be able to become a fully paid-up member and she will be a pretty knowledgeable one at that!

MAY 1988/MARCH 1989

B.H.H.Q. Ltd.

Members visiting Hayes H.Q. during the winter months will have noticed scaffolding around the Clubhouse. This was in support of a major maintenance programme concerned with carrying out remedial work at eaves level to the roof and guttering fascia boards. Also the rear wall has been treated to overcome the damp patches on the Clubroom wall. All this work has now been completed, let's hope we have no more water problems for a few years now.

During the course of this work however it was discovered that the feet of a high proportion of the rafters were in a very poor condition due to dry rot and woodworm. Also those on the front of the building had been partly eaten by squirrels. Many will remember hearing them running around in the roof space before the trees were cut down! Although repairs have been made they are only of a somewhat temporary nature and it will be necessary to overhaul the roof in the next 5-10 years.

MAY 1988/MARCH 1989

Centennial Water-polo Match. Blackheath v Ranelagh.

On the 11th November, in the hundredth anniversary year of our previous match against Ranelagh (away) Blackheath held its return, home fixture at Crystal Palace.

The small area of the diving pool helped the players to conserve energy but the depth of five metres allowed no crafty standing!

The game was hard fought all the way with two goals each in the middle part of the contest. Both sides owed a great deal to their goalies. The tension was eased when Blackheath built a three goal lead towards the end reflecting our stamina built, perhaps, in training for the event.

The Ranelagh team suggested another game soon. The respective Presidents however thought the present frequency about right!

Away match 2088.

MAY 1988/MARCH 1989

"Ron Hill - Who's He?"

You may be aware that Ron Hill completed his 100th marathon two years ago. However Ron's personal and business lives are tied up in running and have been so for many years. It came as quite a surprise therefore when we discovered that a Blackheath Harrier has recently accomplished the same achievement whilst maintaining a job and a family. The man's name is Harry Martin, an ex 100/200m runner, and highlights of Harry's marathons are given below.

"In September 1980 I ran my first marathon in the Masters and Maidens at Guildford finishing in 4 hours 27 minutes. On May 29th 1988 I completed my 100th marathon at Plymouth with a time of 3 hours 37 minutes.

I have actually competed in 104 marathons but dropped out of 4 - Polytechnic/Milton Keynes/Bristol/North Kent.

Unfortunately there is no longer a Milton Keynes or North Kent but I did manage to complete the Poly and the Bristol marathons when I ran them a second time. My personal best time is 3 hours 23 minutes in the 1985 London Marathon.

The most scenic marathons were:
1) New Forest. 2) Galloway (Scotland). 3) Snowdonia.

The easiest were: 1) London. 2) Wolverhampton. 3) Canvey Island.

The toughest were: 1) Snowdonia. 2) Isle of Wight. 3) Pennine/Plymouth.

The most peculiar was the Scilly Isles - 3 large laps and 3 small laps.

I think it is about time I ran an Ultra."

Harry's favourite marathon was West Berlin and apart from competing at 60/70 different venues, he has run in New York (twice), Berlin (twice), Dublin, Moscow, Amsterdam and Rotterdam.

I was running a fair number of marathons at this time and wherever I went, there would be Harry, as he did about one every month. He did not join Blackheath Harriers until he was 43 years old. I remember him as a powerful, big framed man with a large amount of grey/white hair. He was quite a character and may well still be, as I have not heard of his passing. He used to live in Warlingham and would be 90 years old this October, 2022. (Born 15/10/1932).

APRIL/SEPTEMBER 1989

London Marathon. 1989. 23/4/89.

Dear 'heathens,

this year's (1989) Blackheath Harriers' ADT London Marathon Appeal was an outstanding success. The Club set out to raise £5,000 for the Marjorie McClure School for handicapped children at Chislehurst and ended up handing over the magnificent total of £15,100.

This was not the result of any one person's effort but a superb example of Blackheath teamwork. I should like to offer my very sincere thanks to everybody who helped make this appeal a success through their generosity by giving their blood, sweat, tears, time and, not least, money. Our friends at Tiphook PLC made a considerable donation and paid the administration costs of the appeal, which ensured that every penny raised by the runners went to the school.

Yours 'heathenly,

Bill Wheeler. Appeal co-ordinator.

Results

240	Nick Kinsey	2.33.03
427	Roy Smith	2.37.52
585	Dave White	2.40.58
790	B. Mellish	2.44.54
981	Tony Bounds	2.48.07
1096	Roger Morriss	2.49.29
1224	Mike Cronin	2.51.03
1321	Peter Shepheard	2.52.19
1364	Mark Farrell	2.52.52
1377	Duncan Flagg	2.53.04
1378	Mike Lodwig	2.53.05
1404	Stan Ridgewell	2.53.22
1562	John. E. Turner	2.54.58
1762	A. Jones	2.56.49
2068	Mike Peel	2.59.08
2085	Mark Ellison	2.59.13
2195	Ian Wilson	2.59.56
2234	B. O'Gorman	3.00.19

And 46 other Blackheath Harriers finished.

22,587 finished the race.

APRIL/SEPTEMBER 1989

1st April 1989.
Southern 12 Stage Road Relay. Wimbledon Common.
An Historic Occasion Indeed.

We won the Southern 12 Stage Road Relay for the first time in the Club's history. Quite right too, as the long-standing of Blackheath Harriers had stood too long before annexing this title that goes back to its original form as the London to Brighton Road Relay.

Result

1) Blackheath Harriers	4hr 9m 17s
2) Haringey A.C.	4hr 13m 27s
3) Luton United	4hr 13m 53s

The Team:

R. Coles, A. Guilder, T. Linford, J. Barton, G. Arthey, S. Newport, W. Foster, R. Farish, L. Roberts, M. Watling, C. McGeorge and D. Heath.

APRIL/SEPTEMBER 1989

50 Years Membership.

It was Past President Harold Thompson who originally had the idea of a 50-year award, and at a Committee Meeting held on the 7th January 1974 it was agreed "that it would be desirable to mark in some small way fifty years' membership of the club."

It will be noted that the presentation of these souvenirs to some of the members is long overdue. The reason for this has been that it has been impossible to find a manufacturer for the "pots". However, thanks to Past President Peter Stenning, with his knowledge of Goss china, we have decided to replace these "pots" with commemorative dishes.

OCTOBER 1989/MAY 1990
Commonwealth Games.

Congratulations are in order to our two representatives who travelled to New Zealand in January for the Commonwealth Games. Graham Savory and Darrin Morris representing England and Scotland respectively, took seventh and eighth places in the discus throw. Graham with a throw of 57.44 metres and Darrin just behind with 56.10 metres.

OCTOBER 1989/MAY 1990
We'll Keep the Black Flag Flying.

For some years the Club has been sadly short of a pole from which to fly its flag which itself has lain unused as potential moth-fodder.

An estimate was sought for the cost of replacement and an appeal for funds (£300) went out as an insert to the Gazette under the ghastly but topical pun of "pole-tax". Nobody makes such appeals in vain to Blackheathens and the contributions duly began to arrive at Hayes.

However, the President then unexpectedly received a most generous offer from our veteran member Tony Anslow-Wilson. He offered to buy the pole outright as a dedication to the memory of his dear late wife and in the form of a gift that his fellow-members (most of us still unknown to him) might share. Our gratitude for this kind consideration is only equalled by our resolve that somehow, despite his protestation that he rarely feels able to embark on any expedition comparable with a trip to Hayes, we would all do our utmost to bring him to HQ to raise the flag at its first installation.

Meanwhile, I hear you ask, what of the other contributions? Whither they? There is no shortage of good causes, so please withhold them not. Among current favourites for reallocation of the funds is an alphabetical letter-cabinet to help us communicate with each other at HQ, especially at Gazette-issuing times and at Christmas. Also strongly in contention is a pair of replacement gates at the road. Yes, we have an incredible talent for spending money wisely.

OCTOBER 1989/MAY 1990
Some Talk of Alexander, and some of Wooderson....

People often have hobbies that are not only a fascination for themselves but contribute effectively to the sum of human knowledge. An example arose recently when a former colleague of the President's, on hearing the name of Blackheath Harriers, revealed that he had made a lifelong collection of the lyrics of songs sung by troops in the Second World War. Incredibly, he had collected over 2,000 and among those that were printable was one concerning our very own legendary Past President, Sydney Wooderson.

It ran to the tune of a song in the Flanagan and Allen repertoire, "Side by side" and it may help to produce the first verse of the original by way of a reminder of the tune:

"Oh we ain't got a barrel of money
Maybe we're ragged and funny
But we'll travel along
Singin' this song
Side by side."

In the 8th Army version it ran thus (with apologies to our Italian friends for wartime, heat-of-the-moment chauvinism long since evaporated):

"Now, you've heard of Sir Archibald Wavell
The man who made the Eyeties able
To run a mile
In the Wooderson style
Side by side."

On enquiry, Sydney said he knew no more than the rest of us that he was as equally famed in song as story.

OCTOBER 1989/MAY 1990
Getting to the bottom of things....

Another act of generosity stole silently up on the President last winter when four elegant, new, red seated chairs appeared unexpectedly among those on the top table. No bum-numbing, NAAFI-issue, stackers these, but your genuine, horsehair-stuffed, Antiques Roadshow material fit for the most royal of rears.

Past President Ian Wilson seemed to be wearing a knowing look, as well he might; for it appears that a generous offer of the four chairs by Past President Alan Ball had been matched by an equally generous offer by Pauline Wilson to upholster them in red leather conforming with the pattern of the rest of the hospitality chairs ornamenting the President's table.

This remarkable combined operation is typical of the many thoughtful and unheralded acts of kindness performed almost daily for the common good by members and families of our extraordinary society.

OCTOBER 1989/MAY 1990

New York, New York.

The New York Marathon is the ideal stage on which to make a dramatic debut, and Bill Foster certainly managed that the first time he had ever raced over 26 miles 385 yards.

Steve Jones, last year's winner, may have been the first Briton home, but Bill was the first Englishman, despite an unscheduled "pit stop" at 15 miles!

This year's race was run in superb conditions, producing some very fast times. Tanzania's Ikangaa breasted the tape in 2 hours 8 minutes 1 second, with Jones eighth in 2.12.58, having started to drop back between 15 & 16 miles.

Bill crossed the line in Central Park in 22nd place in 2.19.06, the second fastest time ever by a Blackheath Harrier. And but for the emergency stop he could have snatched Bob Richardson's 20 year old record!

It was only a few months ago that Bill ran his first ever half marathon in Guernsey where he was second.

With more experience, he should improve his performance as he was gaining ground and overtaking others in the final leg leading up the hill to the finish in Central Park.

OCTOBER 1989/MAY 1990

An article about member T. E. Hammond.

Long distance walking, now a Cinderella event in athletics, was, in the early part of this century, a great spectator sport; one of its pioneers was T. E. Hamond (1878-1945), "Tommy" to his walking friends.

An illustration of the crowd-pulling power of long distance walking and of Tommy Hammond's tenacity occurred in his record 24-hour walk at the White City Stadium on 11th/12th September, 1908. The distance he covered in the 24 hours was 131 miles, 580 yards, 1 foot, 3 inches; Tommy was prevented from completing the 132nd mile by a boisterous invasion of the track by the capacity crowd.

T. E. Hammond had a history of service to his country as well as to athletics when in 1899 he volunteered for the Boer War and became a cyclist orderly to Lord Kitchener. During the First World War he served for five years (1915-1920) in the Middle East, rising to the rank of Major. After active service he returned to the Stock Exchange where he was made a "member" in 1921 and later founded his own firm of Hammond and Block.

Walking for Tommy was a life-long passion. Years after his record making and breaking walks, he would take his annual holidays by himself striding out over Norway, Finland, the Alps or the Pyrenees.

Amongst his other well-known athletic achievements were: third place in the first Stock Exchange Walk on May 1st 1903. In 1904 he won this event in 8 hours, 26 minutes, 57 seconds - then a record. Later he lowered the record to 8 hours, 18 minutes, 18 seconds.

On June 21st/22nd, 1907, he won the London-to-Brighton-and back Walk in 18 hours, 13 minutes, 37 seconds, making a record which he held for 19 years.

Also in 1907 he made a record from London to Oxford (just under 55 miles) by walking the distance in 8 hours, 51 minutes, 14 seconds. He also held the record for the famous Bradford Walk over a 40 mile course in 6 hours, 37 minutes, 47 seconds.

In 1908 he represented England in the 10,000 metres walk at the Olympic Games, a bit of a sprint for a long distance walker?

In 1914 he created a record for the 42 miles between Norwich and Ipswich.

In an accompanying photo he is wearing a swastika badge on his vest.

For younger members; the motif worn by Tommy Hammond was the emblem of the "Surrey Walking Club" long before a similar logo was adopted by a certain German gentleman.

OCTOBER 1989/MAY 1990

Wacky Races.
The Meltham Maniac Mile.

Long since fed up with running round and round a running track or through ten miles of boring urban concrete, the lads up North have devised a series of races that are spectacular in their conception and innovative in their location, providing a challenge for the runner on the look out for something a little different. There are Fell Races and Mountain Marathons, Round the Walls and Over the Moors, Trans-Pennine Relays and Horseless Horse Trials and then there is the ultimate brush with pain and potential injury, the Uphill and Downhill Mile. Up Mow Cop at 1 in 4 is worthy of the title Killer Mile. Equally so is the series of races that take place downhill at Meltham known as the Maniac Mile.

Take the train from Euston to Manchester Piccadilly, within minutes of being met at the station you're out on the moors. Cross the Pennines into Yorkshire and in less than an hours drive through 'Last of the Summer Wine' country, you arrive at a picturesque stone village nestled in a valley just outside Huddersfield.

A quick change in the Working Men's Institute and you set off up the hill to the start, past shops and stone built houses, past the local Brass Band, past the farms, the fields and finally out onto the moors - when you hit the cattle grid - you've reached the start line.

There's an A and a B race with the C being reserved for non-athletes. Take the A race - it's faster. The only things on your mind now are, will I make it down the hill without falling over and will the first digit on my watch be a 3 when I cross the finish line. The starter sits in the back of a Range Rover thirty yards down the road and after what seems like an eternity blows an air horn to signal the start. He then holds on as the car does a wheelie to escape the sea of runners that threaten to engulf him. Fifty yards down the road and the 'Maniac' in the race title becomes self evident; the breathing's OK but the legs! The legs are running away from you. Each step rams your thigh bones back into your pelvis but any thoughts of slowing or changing direction are immediately dispelled as you realise you are running in perfect synchronisation with the runners directly in front, behind, to the left and to the right.

By half way the field has thinned a little, unbelievably people are getting away from you at the front whilst others have managed to arrest their downward momentum. The pain in your leg joints is excruciating - despite the downhill training and you vow never again. Two hundred to go and although the hill has now increased its angle of descent amazingly you break into a sprint as you pass a couple of 'slower' runners approaching the line. You stop the watch but don't dare to look. But when you do the big 3 is all you look for. And there it is 3.51.47 and you explode with joy and relief. Unless you're the bloke who came all the way up from Yeovil - his watch showed 4.03 - so he'll be back next year.

Back at the institute the beer flows all night and at 65p per pint why shouldn't it. Large baps and pies are 20p each. You and the other 37 sub four minute milers each receive your certificates along with the winner Paul Pickup from Langwood who was just outside the record with 3.32. But the biggest cheer of the night is reserved for the ultimate 'Maniac' Dave Ibbotson, a 34 year old fell-racer from Glossopdale Harriers who took part in all three races and smashed the four minute barrier three times in the space of half an hour. In between, he ran back to the top on each occasion! And I thought I was a bit mad! J. P. (Jim Phelan).

MAY/SEPTEMBER 1990

Subscriptions for 1990/91. New Signing-on Fee.

Subscriptions for the 1990/91 year were due on the first of September 1990. To remind you, the current rates are:

Seniors £25.

Juniors £12.50

Full-time students over 18 on 1st September only pay £12.50

As always, any donations will be gratefully received. This year we need money to offset the general day-to-day expenditure on the Clubhouse. Those of you who subscribe to the Courier know what a great job Bill Clapham is doing. If you would like to receive it, simply add a small donation and you will be included on the next mailing.

Effective from January 1991, a signing-on fee for all new members will apply: Seniors £10. Juniors £5.

MAY/SEPTEMBER 1990

Secretary's Report. 1989/90.

.....An athletics event I was not sure where to slot in was the Triathlon. However, it should be recorded that Nick Kinsey set a British record of 9 hours 5 minutes 20 seconds in the Ironman of Europe event. That was a 2.4 mile swim, 112 miles cycle and a full marathon in 3 hours and 5 minutes.

John Baldwin.

MAY/SEPTEMBER 1990

Track and Field 1990. British League Division One. Match 3. Birmingham. 7th July 1990.

If the British League season had proved to be a bad dream so far, at Birmingham it turned into a fully fledged nightmare.

With a spectacular result required to give us any chance of avoiding relegation, we could only manage last place.

The day had begun with one of the most extraordinary athletic performances of all time, a hammer throw of 1 metre 54cm. With no 'B' string hammer thrower available, Pat Calnan stepped in to throw for a point, and whilst the other throwers held a sweepstake to guess how far he had thrown, Pat retired gracefully to the stand after a job well done. He did come last but so did our 'A' string, Chris Ellis, with 32 metres 96cm!

This does make John E. Turner (me) feel a whole lot better. On the 15th July 2022, at the Vet's match at Tonbridge School, I was sent out to do the Over 50 hammer (aged 72) and managed *5 metres 28cm.*

Well done to Pat. He also did the 3,000m steeplechase and the 400m hurdles.

MAY/SEPTEMBER 1990

Southern League Division Seven. Match One. Norman Park. 5th May. 1990.

.....Steve Freemantle, a last minute recruit turned up and offered to do "anything", this turned out to be both long and triple jumps, combined with the shot and a gruelling 5,000 metre race.

Steve came 4th in the 'A' 5,000 metres in 16.59.00, 3rd in the 'A' triple jump with 10 metres 58cm and 5th in the 'A' string shot with 7 metres 75cm. Jim Phelan the Team Manager was 4th in the 'B' string shot with 6 metres 76 cm.

Jim, sidelined from his usual middle-distance performances by a mid-week calf injury, managed to get in four events too - shot, discus and hammer as well as the oddest high jump event ever witnessed at Norman Park, or perhaps anywhere else for that matter, where 11 of the 13 competitors all cleared the same height, 1 metre 20 cm, and fractions had to be introduced into the scoring as a result of all the 'B' competitors clearing the same height.

Steve also did 4 metres 80 cm in the 'B' string long jump.

MAY/SEPTEMBER 1990

Junior's Summary 1990.

The jigsaw is now complete! Well not quite perhaps. We need some more coaches, a major sponsor, more officials, real ale at the Clubhouse, more cross-country runners for the Kent League etc. etc...., but, as far as the track is concerned a member can join the Club as a colt, move through the Young Athletes' ranks and now find the perfect bridge to the senior ranks. The 1990 season was the Club's first year of having a junior team.

The transition from young athlete to senior has been a minefield for some time. Saturday working; the problems of having to adapt to the use of much heavier senior implements; and the shock for 16 or 17 year olds of suddenly being thrown into competition against athletes twice their age, have all conspired to dampen the enthusiasm and motivation of our younger members. Faced with the consequent high drop-out rate of youngsters a National Junior League was set up by the Old Gaytonians.

MAY/SEPTEMBER 1990

Junior League. Match Three. Croydon.
Sunday 26th August. 1990.

Blackheath used to hold its Club Championships at the Croydon Arena on a circular track that, more often than not, was the consistency of sand when dry and porridge when wet. All that has changed and the new eight-lane tartan track is splendid indeed.

MAY/SEPTEMBER 1990

Great North Run. Newcastle. 16th September 1990.

At only 22 years old, Gary Arthey ran the socks off international rivals in this year's Great North Run, setting a U.K. best time for his age, in what was the fastest half marathon ever run.

The previous day, Mark Steinle, still only 15, finished fourth in the Junior Great North Run, against boys up to three years his senior.

Main result. 30,000 runners.

1st	Steve Moneghetti	60 min. 34 sec
2nd	Douglas Wakiihuri	60 min. 42 sec
8th	Gary Arthey	63 min. 49 sec

SEPTEMBER 1990/APRIL 1991

Ted Pepper Memorial 10K. Park Langley. 6th May. 1991. 108 runners.

The Blackheath Harriers/Paul Davis Associates "Ted Pepper Memorial 10K" was a seven miler until this year, when the course was slightly altered to meet runners' demands for standard metric distances.

Paul Betteridge of Havering A.C. was the winner in 30 minutes 52 secs. 5th was our Dave Hassall in 32.42. and 6th Barry Saddler in the same time. They were followed to the finish by Blackheath's leading V40, Ken Daniel, running in the Club's white summer strip. Seventh position and second veteran in 33 minutes 53 secs. Their combined positions were sufficient to clinch the team prize for Blackheath, well ahead of Cambridge Harriers and Kent A.C.

SEPTEMBER 1990/APRIL 1991

Cambridge Harriers Veteran Road Relay. Rochester Airport. 22nd December. 1990.

It was cold, bleak and windy up above Rochester on the last Saturday before Christmas where four veteran harriers found not only respite from the last Christmas shopping rushes but also a county bronze medal and a couple of pounds of pork chops as prizes. Hugh Morten ran an excellent first leg in 13.13 to bring us 6th place. Jim Phelan, just back from two months of injury, ran just 2 seconds slower and put us in with a medal chance. Peter Hamilton ran the fastest leg of the day for Blackheath (12.58) to take us to 3rd spot where Ken Daniel held us with a leg of 13.16, squeezing Kent A.C. out of the medals. As the meeting was sponsored by a chain of butcher's shops there was meat galore for prizes - definitely not the race for our vegetarian runners!

MAY 1991/MAY 1992

Message from the President. (Alan Pickering).

When debating the proposition that the Club should accept lady members, those attending the Annual General Meeting made sure that every aspect was explored and, in doing so, gave voice to deeply held emotions. To the credit of all concerned, there was a welcome absence of vitriol. Now that the decision has been taken, I sincerely hope that all those who believe that Blackheath Harriers deserves a future which is as illustrious as its past, will play their part in writing what will hopefully be the next exciting chapter in the Club's history. None of the problems which face the Club during this period of transition need be insuperable. Our aim is to ensure that, while offering a warm welcome to new members, existing members must be able to draw from the Club that which encouraged them to join in the first place.

MAY 1991/MAY 1992

Message from the Editor. (Jim Phelan).

Firstly apologies for the delay in the appearance of your Gazette. Fully written up and on course for November 1992 it now finally slithers out almost a year late. Reasons for the delay? Not quite as novel as last year, but equally irksome: our printer parted company with his typesetter, who took his equipment with him thus holding all our copy in limbo for almost a year!

When reading this issue, you will have to cast your minds back a whole two years - forget that we have female members, forget that we are back at Norman Park and all of this will begin to make some sort of sense.

It is summer 1991 and the Juniors finish their first year in Division One of the National Junior League as champions. They went on to take fourth place out of twenty two in the European Juniors Cup in Athens.

MAY 1991/MAY 1992

Sport around the World.

From "The Times" dated February 17th 1992 we glean the following information regarding our overseas division of Blackheath Harriers.

"Athletics: Tim Soutar, a Briton living in Hong Kong, yesterday recorded 2 hours 43 minutes and 26 seconds in the 90°f heat to win the first marathon run in Vietnam."

MAY 1991/MAY 1992

26th October 1991.

Cross-Country Marathon at the Seven Sisters.

Won in 2 hours 45 minutes.

57th	John E. Turner	3hrs 24min
112th	Mike Peel	3 hrs 38min
264th	Brian Hartley	4hrs 3min
288th	Dave Cordell	4hrs 5min
319th	Colin Poole	4hrs 11min
432nd	Denis Lawrie	4hrs 25min
457th	Brian O'Flynn	4hrs 30min
536th	Ian Gold	4hrs 40min
	Don Hopgood (walked)	7hrs 25min

1,470 finished.

MAY 1992/MAY 1993

New President: Stephen Cluney.

Last year we welcomed the Ladies into our midst as successful and competitive equals, this included Tanya Blake gaining her and Blackheath Harriers first Ladies International vest.

This year we take a new step in creating an "Associate Membership" category. With the burgeoning number of teams we field all year, and the loss of officials to the highly competitive Veterans Athletics sphere we, like all clubs, find it increasingly difficult to find sufficient people to manage the Club. Thus we hope to recruit from the Club's followers such as mothers, fathers, wives, husbands and the like, to assist the future development of Blackheath Harriers. Such is the commitment we may ask of some of these people, that we felt it was right that they should be able to be "part of the Club" in their own way. I therefore ask you to welcome these members who are prepared to give their time and effort to help Blackheath Harriers - so that the Club can continue to compete at all levels.

MAY 1992/MAY 1993

Club '5' Cross-Country Championship.
Hayes. 17th October 1992.

Aided, no doubt, by the turn out for the quadrennial Club Photograph (the last all-male edition) and a lovely sunny afternoon, the Club managed to turn out a record 121 competitors for this the oldest of our trophies.

Dave Heath won in a time of 28.46 with Dave Taylor just one second behind. First place in the handicap went to Chris Haines, making a widely welcomed return to something approaching his previous form.

MAY 1992/MAY 1993

Mob Match v Orion Harriers.
Hayes. 28th November 1992.
123 finished.

The race had added historical significance in that it was the first event in which the Club was (legally) represented by female members. Margaret Baldwin was an excellent 49th (much to the chagrin of a large number of regulars) with Sharon Cook and Cath Messent also going the distance.

Margaret Baldwin, Cath Messent, Susan Cluney, Heather Hassall and Jenny Jackson all joined the Club on the 2nd November 1992.

MAY 1992/MAY 1993

Mob Match v South London Harriers.
Coulsdon. 6th February 1993.

....Cath Messent became the first woman to win a handicap event - evidently her "messing-about-at-the-back-looking -half-dead" act in the previous match had fooled the Hon. handicapper completely.

MAY 1992/MAY 1993

Women's Cross-Country.

With the first women having been admitted to the Club as recently as the 2nd November 1992, it is hardly surprising that we have yet to make an impact on the Cross-Country scene. However, in the Southern Women's Championships, held on 17th January 1993 at Bedford, we were represented in the Inters race by Rachel Porte (86th) and in the Seniors by Cath Messent (172nd).

A month later in the National Women's Championships at Luton on the 20th February 1993, Cath Messent (340th) and Rona Smith (506th) ensured that the blue and white intertwined squares were seen for the first time on the national women's stage. With the continuing growth of our female membership, next year will be a different story.

MAY 1993/MAY 1994

Editorial.

....The ladies completed their first ever summer season by finishing 6th in the Kent Women's League and look forward to more successes in the future as their membership figures rise.

....On the roads, we gained our first ever National Relay title in the National Six Stage Championship at Aldershot in October and then in December picked up the AAA of England 10Km Road Race Championship title in Leeds.

....In the London Marathon Bill Foster took the 21 year old Club record off Bob Richardson when he finished 29th in 2.17.15 and then knocked another second off it in the European Championships later in the year.

....In January we confirmed our progress by again finishing first in the South of England Cross-Country Championships at Parliament Hill, this time with a resounding 77 points victory over Shaftesbury. But our greatest triumph of the Winter season took place at South Shields on 12/3/1994 where a triumphant Blackheath defeated the best in the country to win the National Cross-Country title for the first time in our 125 year history. On the Friday evening the Shaftesbury team with whom we shared a hotel informed us following their inspection, that the course was undulating and very dry, this brought smiles to the faces of a number of our team.

The feeling was that a medal was possible, the colour remained to be seen, but the team's spirit was one of quiet confidence and determination. Captain, Mark Watling's last act was to drop himself from the squad, he was about to see history unfold. Pre-race favourites were Bingley, with their pursuers likely to be local Morpeth Harriers, Shaftesbury, Blackheath and the ever dangerous Tipton.

It was a 3 lap course that was excellent for spectators, but where it traversed footpaths a cinder and ash material had been spread, which was to cause many contestants to finish the day with shoes full of a coagulated mess of ash, blood and blisters. The race was fast and furious throughout. Spencer Newport, after a disappointing run in the Southern, was undoubtedly firing on all cylinders, as he edged ever closer to the top ten. Strongman Dave Taylor got faster as the race progressed, but was being hotly pursued only a few places back by Darrell Smith, while native North Eastener Steve Dodd was battling it out a few yards behind with Mark Colpus and Jerry Barton in close attendance. That for anyone who can count very rapidly made up the scoring six. Still storming through, after his normal cautious start was marathoner Alan Guilder, well supported by Roy Smith and Giles Clifford.

With one mile to go the Morpeth Team Manager informed us that he had 5 in the first 26 places, he added that his sixth scorer was outside the first one hundred finishers. He then conceded defeat as he scurried away.

The result:

Spencer Newport	8th
Dave Taylor	14th
Darrell Smith	16th
Steve Dodd	38th
Jerry Barton	41st
Mark Colpus	54th

The team was completed by:

Alan Guilder	74th
Roy Smith	194th
Giles Clifford	255th

1st	Blackheath Harriers	171 points
2nd	Bingley Harriers	203 points
3rd	Morpeth Harriers	214 points

The following Wednesday at Hayes HQ it was standing room only as well over 100 people crowded into the Clubhouse for the arrival of the National Trophy. (Actually the Frank Wynne Trophy.) The celebrations went on well into the early hours of the following morning.

For the Women, Tanya Blake finished first in the Kent and Southern Inter-Counties Cross-Country Championships, third in the Southerns at Parliament Hill and an excellent fourth in the U.K. World Cross-Country trials at Alnwick. Having gained selection for the Great Britain team she went on to finish 77th in the World Cross-Country Championships in Budapest.

How a club with so much success across the board in all ages and sexes on track and country fails to attract a major sponsor is beyond understanding. But with Steve Cluney (President) now on the case, that major omission could well be rectified as his extended year in office (to bring about a more manageable January to December Club year) has coincided with our most successful Winter to date. May his search for a sponsor prove every bit as fruitful.

MAY 1994/MAY 1995

Subscription fees for 1996.

Seniors £36 + £10 joining fee.

Under 20s and full-time students £20 + £5 joining fee. This is only available to persons who have never been full members of the Club.

MAY 1994/MAY 1995

English National Cross-Country Championships. Luton. 11th March 1995.

You know what they say about buses. You can wait 124 years and then suddenly you win the National twice. We had 6 runners finish in the top 40. It was a 14Km race won in 43 minutes 43 seconds by Spencer Duval.

We had:

6th	D. Taylor	45.13
9th	T. Dickinson	45.26
11th	S. Newport	45.34
27th	S. Dodd	46.27
28th	P. Hogston	46.29
39th	S. Baines	47.02

The best team score since 1946.

MAY 1994/MAY 1995

AAA Women's Road Relays. Sutton Coldfield. 12th November. 1994.

The Club's women's section won its first ever National medals when the Under 13 team finished third. Star of the team was Gemma Viney who on the last leg moved the team up from 9th to 3rd, running the equal fastest time of the day.

Team:
Katie Lucht, Zoe Morrell and Gemma Viney.

MAY 1994/MAY 1995

AAA of England Half Marathon Championship. Wilmslow. 19th March 1995.

Blackheath Harriers senior men took their second National title in 9 days when they won the Half Marathon Championships in Cheshire.

Such is the Club's strength that none of the four man team were among the six who won the National Cross-Country title.

The winner was Andy Green of Warrington in 64 minutes 39 seconds. Second placer, our Bill Foster, finished in a new pb of 64 minutes and 46 seconds. In 4th place was Alan Guilder in 66.15. 11th was Mark Colpus in 68.30 and 26th was Dave Lee in 72.46.

MAY 1994/MAY 1995

Southern 12 Stage Road Relay. Thurrock. 9th April 1995.

We won this Championship for only the second time in the Club's history. The team this time was: Steve Dodd, Mark Watling. Simon Baines, Roy Smith, Chris Wada, Pat Calnan, Dave Taylor, Mark Steinle, Phil Hogston, Andrew Hollens, Dave Lee and Daren Neale.

National 12 Stage Road Relay. Sutton Coldfield. 29th April 1995.

Not only had we won this coveted title, but we had done so with panache. Dave Lee brought us home almost three minutes ahead of Bingley and Morpeth.

The team was: Hogston, Dodd, Dickinson, Guilder, D. Smith, S. Baines, D. Taylor, M. Steinle, J. Harrison, S. Newport, W. Foster and D. Lee.

SUMMER 1995/WINTER 1995/6

Editorial.

Dear 'Heathens,

As you can see we have ventured into the glossy world of modern type setting and colour printing in an attempt to bring the Gazette back to centre-stage within the Club.

Cover photo: Julian Golding and Linford Christie by Andre Camara, the Times. This photograph accompanied an article on Monday June 5th 1995 entitled "Golding confident he can bridge senior gap."

To begin with we shall be producing 2 Gazettes a year at six monthly intervals. The deadline once set, will be adhered to irrespective of what copy has been received.

Blackheath Courier.

The Courier appears six times a year (Sept,, Nov, Jan, Mar, May, July) for those members who wish to take it. Both current and back issues can always be collected at HQ from the 'Courier Box' near the main downstairs noticeboard, kindly provided by Brian Saxton.

SUMMER 1995/WINTER 1995/6.

October began well for John E. Turner when he again completed the London to Brighton race and to prove that he is currently the Club's leading exponent of ultra-distance running he acquitted himself very well in the Sri Chinmoy 24 hour track race, which by his own description sounds like the ultimate masochistic nightmare. 1996 has continued in much the same vein for John, with 3 marathons completed in 13 days in April, averaging 3 hours 7 minutes each.

It is such fun, when you can put yourself, in your own book.

SUMMER 1995/WINTER 1995/6
The National Cross-Country Championships.

Newark in 1996 saw the first totally 'open' National, and many new 'heathen faces got the chance to run with the best. Two coach (and several car) loads of supporters made the trip to participate in this tremendous celebration of our sport.

After our total annihilation of the cream of the country's Cross-Country teams last year at Luton it was, perhaps inevitable that we could not pull it off again. We just had too many of our best absent, unfit, or just generally out-of-sorts. The strengthened Bingley team produced the sort of performance we did last year, to take the title just as convincingly. Nevertheless, showing tremendous strength of character, our team (which knew right from the start it was not doing well) gave it its best shot. Spencer Newport ran well in 13th place. Dave Taylor (20th), Bill Foster (24th), Tim Dickinson (26th), Chris Wada (134th) and Darrell Smith (144th) completed the scoring. Other finishers were Steve Dodd (170th), Pat Calnan (194th), Paddy Brice (206th), Giles Clifford (244th), Roy Smith (258th), Steve Pairman (1085th), Nick Barber (1612th), Steve Freemantle (1682nd), John E. Turner (1683rd), Wilf Orton (1792nd) and Derek Dhammaloka (1922nd). Of these, the latter 6 all recorded personal bests!

And so it was that we were 1st in an altogether novel way - the first club ever to finish 3rd in 3 consecutive Nationals at Newark! Let us see Bingley try that one....

SUMMER 1995/WINTER1995/6
Plan 2000.

During 1995 the Club's Development Committee considered, among other matters, a Five Year Plan for the Club. In December the General Committee approved the "Plan 2000" and in March it was presented to the members at the Annual General Meeting.

The 5 Year Plan is intended to focus strategic objectives of the Club as a whole. It should be a living thing - reviewed every year, allowing for revised plans to be re-written on a rolling basis. As a means of focussing on what the Club is all about, a Mission Statement sets the theme for the Plan.

WE AIM to excel together
Through the fulfilment of each member's own athletic potential.
For the benefit of the sport as a whole.

WE PURSUE the highest standards of:
Coaching, organisation and fair-play
In all our activities.

WE RESPECT competition and friendship
Individuals and teams
Winners and all participants.
Club records and personal bests.
....in a word: "CLUBMANSHIP"

SUMMER 1995/WINTER 1995/6
The Club 10 mile Cross-Country - Or is it?
By Steve Freemantle

The Club 10 Cross-Country race has, I imagine, been run for over a hundred years over various terrain in and around south-east London. Without the time to delve deep into the Club history books (shame, I hear you say!), I am not sure how long the race has been held in its present form; certainly it has been run on the same course since I joined the Club some 12 years ago.

During my enforced absence from active athletics in the 95/96 Cross-Country season, I had the opportunity using equipment kindly purchased by my employers to correctly measure the said Club 10 mile course. The results follow.

Start: Near the Old Cafe.

Entry into the woods 245 metres

Junction of Baston Manor Road/West Common Road 705 metres.

- another 22 points are listed with the measurements.

Then - Finish: Near the Old Cafe.
Total Distance 15,727 metres

So, with my elementary maths, I conclude that the Club 10 is actually the Club 9 + 1,243 metres, some 366 metres short of the full distance, but what's that between friends!

Don Hopgood may find an extra field for us to run around in 1997.

SUMMER 1996/WINTER 1996/7
Mike Mahoney. President. 1997/1998.

....The challenge of being the President for the next 12 months really excites me. I have no theme for the year or any great desire to instigate revolutionary change. I am a supporter of tradition which is something we have plenty of and is after all what gives the Club its unique character. We would do well to remember however, that today's traditions were yesterday's innovations. We must be ready to embrace change when it is necessary if we are to move forward and develop. Blackheath is a forward looking club and we will soon be pushing the boundaries still further with our own dedicated website on the Internet. Just the start we need to take us into the next century.

SUMMER 1996/WINTER 1996/7
Young Athletes.

....The boys once again did a fantastic job in not only bringing home our 8th National Young Athletes title but by the largest margin in the history of the league.

SUMMER 1996/WINTER 1996/7
Obituaries. L. E. Hammill.

....Past President Laurie Hammill died in September 1995 aged 89.

....It was Laurie's idea that a Vice-President's supper should be held so that the V.P.s might meet the new President and Vice-Presidents early after their election. The first supper that he had arranged at the "Two Chairmen" in Westminster occurred five days after his installation as President in October 1962, hence he became the chief guest at his own feast.

....As a prodigious walker he would think nothing of walking from his home at Blackheath to Rochester to attend a County committee meeting, to Coulsdon for a mob match or up to London and many other similar venues, on one occasion he walked to Croydon to visit a Club member in hospital.

SUMMER 1996/WINTER 1996/7
Loofah Appeal for the Ladies' Shower Room.

Contributions have been gratefully received. Total donated so far £774!

WINTER 1996/SPRING 1997
London Youth Games Cross-Country. Parliament Hill.

Of the 39 young athletes representing the London Borough of Bromley in the six races, no less than 30 were from Blackheath. A small piece of athletics history was made as it was the first time in the event's history that all 32 London Boroughs (33 including the City of London) entered teams. Bromley finished second to Havering last year, and the youngsters were hoping to go one better this year. So on a glorious if rather cold, winter morning swords were crossed for what proved to be a close fought contest.

Overall borough positions:

1st	Havering.	268.
2nd	Bromley.	255.
3rd	Harrow.	247.

WINTER 1996/SPRING 1997
Success on the roads.

1997 was an excellent year for the Club over the longer distances on the roads. Blackheath Harriers featured strongly at the AAA's Half-Marathon Championships in Reading and at the AAA's Marathon Championships in London, where we won silver medals in the team competitions.

The Half-Marathon was held on a cold, windy day in March and no-one wanted to push the early pace. A group of 10 were bunched together at the 11 mile mark, reached in 55.14, at which point the race really began. A 12th mile in 4.36 reduced the group to four, with Spencer Duval, Dave Tune, Mark Steinle and Bill Foster having broken away. At this point, Spencer Duval put his foot down and covered the next mile in 4.27, opening up a small gap on Mark and Bill which he held to the finish. Mark took second place and looks to have a very bright future at the marathon when he eventually moves up.

Final result.

1st	Spencr Duval.	64.50.
2nd	Mark Steinle.	64.56.
3rd	Bill Foster.	64.57.

Our success in Reading set us up for the London Marathon on the 13th April. Conditions on race day were excellent, warm but not too hot and no wind. It turned out to be a great day for the Club, with the first four 'Heathens to finish totalling 10 hours 22 minutes and 35 seconds, which took the silver medals behind Sunderland. This is the first time the Club has taken team honours since the London began in 1981. The scoring four were:

Bill Foster	2.18.44.
Roy Smith.	2.28.30.
Richard Parrott.	2.37.27.
Nick Kinsey.	2.37.55.

WINTER 1996/SPRING 1997
Blackheath Harriers Ladies Brooches. Now available.

Specially hand crafted jewellery in hallmarked sterling silver.

Approximate size: New 50p piece.

Priced at £25 each (inc P&P).

Also available in 9ct gold subject to special order.

Cuff-links and earrings also available subject to demand.

Silver Blackheath Brooch	£25.
Silver Cuff-links	£33.
Silver Blackheath Earrings	£33.
Silver Blackheath Tie Clip	£30.
Gold Blackheath Brooch	£90.

SUMMER 1997/WINTER 1997/8
AAA 10,000m Championships. Bedford. 25th May 1997.

Mark Steinle became the Club's first ever AAA's 10,000m champion when he ran away from the field with six laps to go. Initially no-one went with him and he quickly built up a thirty metre lead. His nearest challenger was Dave Taylor, who closed the gap over the last lap, but it wasn't quite enough. So the Club secured both the gold and silver medals.

1st	Mark Steinle.	29.27.98.
2nd	Dave Taylor.	29.29.59.

SUMMER 1997/WINTER 1997/8
AAA Decathlon Championships. Sheffield. 31st May-1st June 1997.

Alexis Sharp totally dominated this, seizing the initiative from the start, he led all the way, achieving his best point scores in the 100m, 400m, long jump and 110m hurdles.

Results:

100m	11.00.
Long jump	7.23m.
Shot	12.45m.
High Jump	1.77m.
400m	48.57.
110m hurdles	15.01.
Discus	43.72m.
Pole Vault	3.90m.
Javelin	60.68m.
1500m	4.57.01.

SUMMER 1997/WINTER 1997/8
Vets report - Summer 1997.

Individually the highlight of the late summer was Hugh Morten's marvellous British age best One Hour run at Norman Park on 3rd September when the 49 year old super athlete covered 17,292 metres - approx. 10¾ miles at 5 minute 35 second pace! Well done to Hugh.

SUMMER 1997/WINTER 1997/8
South of England Cross-Country Championships. Parliament Hill. 31st January. 1998.

Our scoring six finished inside the first fifty to regain comfortably the team title and record the fifth win in six years.

SUMMER 1997/WINTER 1997/8
London to Brighton.
Sunday 5th October 1997.

Sunday 5th October was another special day in the history of the Club. The first London to Brighton took place in 1951. It starts at 7a.m. on Westminster Bridge and yet at 6.45 you wouldn't believe that anything was about to happen; you wonder if you are in the right place. The field of 120 then appear from nowhere and on the first stroke of 7 from Big Ben, they're off.

Our team is numbered 1 to 6; it includes John E Turner who does it every year, Colin Poole who is starting for the third time and Alan Jones for the second time. Trevor Wood, Gareth Griffin and Brian Smith are first timers. John has always wanted to be part of a Blackheath team in this event. Will this be the year?

During 1997 the age range for our Southern League Division 7 team was from 16 to 65. For the London to Brighton it was from 18 to 60? Who said there is a generation gap?

Four finished with Trevor Wood leading us home in 8 hours and 26 minutes. Gareth came in 12 minutes later, just 2 minutes ahead of John. Over an hour later Brian Smith came home in 9 hours and 44 minutes. With 4 to score, we finished a team for the first time for many years. They were rewarded with SEAA Championship medals as the event had hosted the 1997 SEAA Ultra Distance Championships.

The previous week we had celebrated the success of our Juniors in the European Juniors Club Cup. This week we celebrated another remarkable achievement by a junior member of the Club.

18 months previously Gareth Griffin had cancer and was undergoing treatment, including radiotherapy at St. Thomas' Hospital, so you can imagine his thoughts as he passed that hospital immediately after the start of this race. The treatment was successful, the results showing that he has fully recovered his health. He ran to prove how well he was, he ran in an attempt to beat his Dad's best time of 8 hours and 42 minutes and he ran to raise money for the Macmillan Cancer Appeal. How brilliantly he performed. At the top of Ditchling Beacon he had 57 minutes to do the last six miles and his Dad said "It's all down to pride now." He made it with 4 minutes to spare.

At the main presentation Gareth was presented with a cut-glass tankard, a gift from St. Thomas' Hospital. On it is inscribed 'Gareth Griffin, what an inspiration.' After his story was told he was given a standing ovation with not many dry eyes in the house. He had rightly worn Number One in the race. He was duly acclaimed the following Wednesday at the Club where he deservedly received his second standing ovation.

Our Club History and our Gazettes tell us that we won the individual and team awards in the first two London to Brighton races. Lew Piper and Derek Reynolds may have run faster over the old, shorter and flatter course, but they would certainly be very proud of their 1997 successors as should we all.

SUMMER 1997/WINTER 1997/8
Sri Chinmoy 24 Hour Race.
Tooting Bec Track. 12th & 13th October. 1997.

Having won a South of England AA team medal in the London to Brighton race the previous weekend, John E Turner was only a mile and two places away from an individual National Championship medal in the 24 hour race at Tooting Bec. It rained for 18 of the 24 hours but John was still very close to the personal best he had set two years previously. In reasonable conditions he would surely have added 15 to 20 miles to the excellent 116 miles 377 yards he ran.

The President was amongst the many Blackheath visitors to Tooting Bec who were appalled by the cold, wet and windy conditions but amazed by the competitors' bravery. Nonetheless there was a very warm welcome at the temporary home erected by the

Griffins at Tooting Bec. Such was the size of this erection that one wondered whether planning permission had been necessary. Such was the amount of alcohol that flowed in their establishment surely a licence had also been needed. The beds and other creature comforts that the 'mansion' contained brought the word 'bordello' to mind. Then I looked it up in the dictionary! Perhaps not! By Mike Martineau.

I (John) saw it a bit differently. There was a large tent at the side of the track and the sides of it would sway to music. Also coming from inside of it was singing, laughing and the clinking of glasses as I laboriously did yet another lap on the flooded track! Every few laps the entrance zip would come down a few feet and a hand with a glass of beer or gin would be thrust out with a "Go on John" and then up went the zip again. Thanks for the support my jolly Club mates. Well, I suppose you pay your money, you do what you want! How I wanted to get in that tent but luckily they wouldn't let me.

Sheila Griffin relates her own recollections of a "weekend away with Dick".

The Lobotomy Run. (A night out with the lads).

My husband travels abroad fairly frequently and being a kind, thoughtful and generous man, he often brings me back lovely gifts or arranges a surprise treat for me instead. This usually takes the form of a no-expense-spared meal at the local Harvester (get there at 5 o'clock and get a third off) but this offer, one balmy evening in the summer nearly took my breath away.

"Darling", he whispered in my ear, "Let me take you away for the weekend. I've got just the place in mind. It's only open to a very select number, we can spend the night under the stars, watching the ever-changing panorama as the first fingers of dawn kiss the early morning dew. There will be exotic foods, stimulating drinks and last but not least, me, half naked and giving everything to my performance!" "How can I refuse?" I replied all a-quiver. "Leave everything to me beloved, I'll make it a weekend to remember." He is so masterful at times.

The weekend extravaganza was planned for the 11th and 12th of October and as the date approached I turned a deaf ear to furtive phone calls and ignored the mad dash to reach the mail each morning. On Friday evening, full of eager anticipation, I carefully packed my overnight case with a slinky, satin nightie and a large bottle of Obsession (what more does a girl need?) and then my hero came up to me and said, "I think you might need these!" I looked in astonishment at the pile of jumpers, leggings, socks, boots, hats and waterproofs that he had dumped at my feet but just then I caught a glimpse of his favourite New Balance shoes peeking cheekily out of his bag and a terrible suspicion leapt into my mind. "You wouldn't by any chance be thinking of going for a run some time this weekend would you?"

I must admit; Richard did have the grace to look sheepish as he nodded and mumbled, "Not just for a bit of it, I'm afraid, all of it - it's the Sri Chinmoy 24 Hour Track Race at Tooting Bec. All the food is ready and I've hooked the trailer tent up to the car. There's loads of bananas and Isostar drink for you to make up and best of all we've got smelly eggy sandwiches!" He looked so pleased with himself that all I could do was smile sweetly and seethe inwardly.

We arrived at the track at 10 a.m. Saturday and were really lucky to get a prime position, just next to the 'doggy-do' bin, beneath a floodlight and in direct line of fire from the pigeons roosting overhead. Richard laid out his kit of 2 pairs of gloves, 4 hats, 8 T-shirts, 4 vests, 3 pairs of shorts, 2 tracksters and a waterproof jacket to which he attached the number 26.

I was shown where I could get hot drinks and where the hot food would be served - slimy pasta - yuk! More importantly I found the one warm place in the whole of the arena - the loos!

The tension was mounting as the time came for the 45 runners to make their way to the start line and then suddenly they were off - tearing around the track at a break-neck speed of 3 m.p.h. The rain fell, the thunder rolled and still those athletes ran on and on and on.

The growing crowd of spectators (at least 10 by now) were almost whipped to a frenzy in anticipation of the next highlight; after 4 hours the runners changed direction. The excitement was intense, would they manage it or would it prove just too much for these poor, tortured souls? Hurrah! They all came through safely without loss of life or injury to limb and some even had the strength to wave.

So the pattern continued until 2 a.m., the heavens poured down freezing, driving rain, the wind increased to gale force and just to cap it all, the zip on the tent door broke, allowing all the elements to come in and join me.

By now, Richard's brain was completely anaesthetised by the cold and it was a simple job to coax him into the tent with the promise of a steaming cup of Bovril and once there, to pounce on him, bundle him into a sleeping bag and thaw him out in the arms of Morpheus for a couple of hours.

A friendly race marshal called him at 4.30 a.m. and, looking awful but smelling even worse, Richard stumbled his way back on to the track. Around 9 a.m. the weather changed for the better - even the sun managed to come out and peer in disbelief at the spectacle unfolding beneath its warming rays.

At long last, the hooter sounded at noon to mark the end of the gruelling run and Richard staggered back to the tent after completing 72 miles.

He sat shaking with his Bacofoil blanket wrapped around his exhausted frame and as I peeled off his soaking wet socks and lovingly tended his blisters, I had to ask, "Why do you do it?" A true runner, he replied, "For fun of course!"

SUMMER 1997/WINTER 1997/8
Blackheath Harriers Golf Society.

The Society was formed on an informal basis in the spring of 1997 as it had been noticed that there were now about twenty members who played golf. The idea was to give members both a break from their intensive training programmes (ha ha!) and the opportunity of a pleasant walk in congenial company and further, to try to refute the argument that golf is a long walk interspersed with disappointment.

The inaugural meeting was held on the 3rd July 1997 on the Old Championship Course at Addington Court under the Stableford scoring system (ask Bill Clapham for an explanation). Conditions were wet, but the rain stayed away. Members taking part were Tony Pontifex, Steve Freemantle, Brian O'Flynn, Jonathan Brown, Brian Hartley, Dick Griffin, Past President Don Gillate, John Hills, Mike Lodwig and Barry Shapcott.

Brian O'Flynn took the opening drive and was no doubt relieved to see it go straight down the fairway. Other tee shots had mixed results with Mike Lodwig hitting a colossal drive well out of bounds. Thereafter, he hardly put a foot wrong returning a gross score of 84 to be the clear winner with 43 Stableford points. Not bad for a player whose official handicap is 26! Tony Pontifex was second with 35 points and Brian O'Flynn third with 33 points. The wooden spoon was won by John Hills with 5 points! Despite the doubtful conditions everybody had enjoyed themselves and it was therefore decided to have an afternoon at Kingsdown near Dover, where Don Gillate is a member, on the 11th of September.

Eight members and three guests took part and we were joined for the first time by Graham Fee and Denis Lawrie. Kingsdown is a very hilly course and with the wind blowing strongly it was a tough test of golf, added to which there was also another society on the course which led to very slow play. However the result was much closer than in the previous competition. There was a tie on 33 points for first place between Brian O'Flynn and Mike Lodwig (despite his handicap being cut by 4 points). Brian eventually being adjudged the winner on the strength of a better last nine holes. Brian Hartley came third on 32 points with a further 4 players within 2 points of Brian. This time the wooden spoon went to professional photographer Barry Shapcott with 12 points. A most congenial evening was spent in the clubhouse, and thanks must go to Don Gillate for organising such an excellent day. Following the success of these two meetings, it is hoped to arrange similar events, so if there are any latent golfers in the Club please get in touch with either Tony Pontifex or Steve Freemantle.

SPRING/SUMMER 1998

Active athletics is what the Club is all about and 1997 had far more successes than disappointments. At the very highest level Julian Golding had his best ever year winning a bronze medal at the World Championships when anchoring the 4x100 men's relay team. He also won the European under 23 200m Championship and re-wrote the Club 200m record. At the European Junior Championships Emeka Udechuku won the discus and Mark Findlay also collected a gold in the 4x100m relay to add to his bronze in the 200m. Mark Steinle represented Great Britain in the World Student Games half-marathon finishing an excellent 6th, the first non-African! With Dave Taylor he then represented Great Britain in the World Half-Marathon Championships. Dave ran a personal best of 63.24 to finish 53rd. This pair were also 1st and 2nd in the AAA's 10K, Mark leading Dave home by less than 2 seconds. This was the Club's first ever AAA's 10K win. Dave also claimed the Club Marathon record when he ran 2.13.27 in Frankfurt.

SPRING/SUMMER 1998
Obituaries.
John Anderson.

We have only recently learnt of the death a few years ago of life member, John Anderson, of whom little is known though he had corresponded with the Club some ten years ago and had attended a members' night at Hayes a year or two before he died. He had been a member of the Club more years than any other, nearly eighty, having been elected in 1915 at the age of 8. He was proposed by his father, also a life member, who had been elected in 1897, thus creating a family link with the Club of around a century, a tribute to them both in itself.

A member had visited John's home, White Lodge Cottage, Upper Norwood, after a letter addressed to him from the Club had been returned by the Post Office as "Gone Away". A few enquiries amongst neighbours, some of whom remembered John, established that he had died three or four years before. Although the cottage had lain derelict for those years, the Post Office continued to deliver correspondence for all that time. It was only when the premises were raised to the ground for back-land development that our last letter was returned.

AUTUMN/WINTER 1998/99
Secretary's Report. 1998.

The undoubted individual star of the year was Julian Golding. He started the year in impressive indoor form, winning the AAA title in 20.46 seconds. This form continued into the outdoor season and the highlight came in the Commonwealth Games 200m final, when a majestic run won him the gold medal in a world class time of 20.18.

SPRING/SUMMER 1999
Vets Track and Field Report. 1999

Top marks must go to Gordon Hickey, winning a bronze in the Over 65 shot at the World Championships and also breaking the British record at the Southern Counties Vets A.C. Champs in June (13.30m).

At the World's, Bill Foster came 6th in the 5,000m (15.01), Dennis Wallington 10th in the Long Jump (5.63m), Sean Lightman 8th in the 20K walk (1.57.15) and Bob Minting made the semi's in the 800m.

Earlier in the year Dennis Wallington won gold in the BVAF Championships jumping 5.76m. At the same meeting

Jim Day secured three gold medals and two silver medals!

SPRING/SUMMER 1999

Triathlete Nick Kinsey wins the National Vets (40-45) Mountain Bike Champs and is competing in the BUPA Brighton Triathlon where he hopes to qualify for the "Worlds" which are in Perth in 2000.

AUTUMN/WINTER 1999/2000
Press release. 26/3/2000.

World famous Blackheath Harriers has started the new century by changing its name for the first time in 122 years. At Saturday's Annual General Meeting, the membership voted to rename the Club, Blackheath Harriers Bromley.

The change is not revolutionary, but a recognition of the status quo, as the Club has been based in the Bromley area for 80 years, firstly from 1921 in West Wickham and then from 1926 at Hayes. The Club was formed in 1869 as Peckham Hare and Hounds and changed it's name when it moved to Blackheath in 1878.

The 1990's proved to be the most successful decade in the Club's history with the Senior Men winning the National Cross-Country and the National 12 Stage Relays for the first time. The Juniors were seven times National Junior Athletic League Champions; and eight National Young Athletes Finals were won. Numerous athletes have gained international recognition with the highlight being Julian Golding's win in the 200 metres at the 1998 Commonwealth Games.

AUTUMN/WINTER 1999/2000
European Indoor Championships. Ghent. 25th-27th February.

Julian Golding became the Club's first ever winner of a medal at the European Indoor Championships when he finished 3rd in the 200 metres. He qualified for the final with second places in both his heat and semi-final with times of 20.96 and 20.87 and found himself drawn in lane 3 for the final. For much of the race it looked like he would replicate his 4th place from 2 years ago but with Cypriot Anninos Marcoullides pulling up with an injury on the final bend, Julian swept through to take the bronze medal.

AUTUMN/WINTER 1999/2000
**Cross-Country Season.
The Club Championships.
The Club 5 miles.
23rd October 1999. Hayes.**

A smaller turn out than usual with 51 starters for the Club 5 opened the home fixtures for the year. Ever present Roy Smith appeared to have the Senior race all his own way in the absence of any elite squad members there to test out their early season fitness. He won in 29.01.

The Club 7½ miles. 27th November 1999. Chingford.

Result:

1st	Roy Smith	47.00.
2nd	John Beck	49.37.
3rd	Andy Lawes	51.44.

**The Club 10 miles.
4th March 2000. Hayes.**

Result:

1st	Roy Smith	63.17.
2nd	John Morland	66.28.
3rd	A storming run from over 50 veteran Hugh Morten	67.10.

Subsequent research showed that Roy was only the fifth member to have ever won all three titles in the same season, the last being our current President, Richard Coles, over twenty years ago.

SPRING/SUMMER 2000
AAA's 10,000m Trial. Watford. 22/7/2000.

Mark Steinle posted his second Olympic qualifying time when he finished 4th in the AAA's Olympic 10,000 metre trial at Watford. Already selected for Great Britain in the marathon, his time of 28.04.48 was nearly six seconds inside the qualifying mark. It also breaks the

Club record of Bob Richardson, which has stood since 1969, by 31 seconds, a second for every year. A new best by over a minute, Steinle was also pleased with the negative splits. "I ran the first 5,000 in 14.04 and the second half in 13.59 which is only a second off my 5km best." Although 3rd Briton home in the race, he was not seeking double Olympic selection, happy to be doing the marathon.

SPRING/SUMMER 2000
Visit to Sydney and Stanley Wooderson.
Written by Richard Coles.

It was my great pleasure to travel to Wareham in Dorset on 21st June 2000 to meet Sydney and Stanley Wooderson, especially since only a few days earlier Sydney had been awarded the MBE in the Queen's birthday honours list. The talk over lunch ranged widely over the last 70 years of athletics, the progress of the world mile record and Sydney's many fine races.

Interestingly I did not see a single photograph of Sydney racing in his home. I wonder how many World mile record holders you could say that about! He was concerned that he wouldn't recognise the Clubhouse anymore but I assured him that he would instantly feel at home in the Clubroom and in the changing rooms, which in essence have not changed.

He reminisced about Club Mob Matches and the delights of our 5 and 7½ mile cross-country courses and Ladywell track.

Unfortunately he finds the walks he used to enjoy in Wareham Forest beyond him now, but with assistance to climb the steps over the back garden fence he walks on the common land to the rear of their bungalow every day, weather permitting. Sydney does not like to travel much, he says he can't see the point, as he can't see much. However, with the support of his family he thinks he might make the journey to Buckingham Palace to receive his award.

The Pack Sweeps on Together

With thanks to: Peter "the Jogle Brother" Rogers and Sue Rogers, Maz Turner, Dave and Caroline Leal, Nick Barber, Andy Edwards, Nic Corry, Ozzie Adams, Tim Ayres, David Appleton, Fred Stuart, Roger Beswick, Iain Swatton, Bob Minting, Helen Godsell, Andy Tucker, Nick Mayers, Roger Pinder, George Collins, Chris Haines, Pat Calnan, Bill and Jo Clapham, Jim Phelan, Cliff Keen, Mike Peel, Tom Phillips, Dave White, Paul Sharpe, Deniz Mehmed, Clayton Aves, Jackie and Ian Montgomery, Anne Cilia and Mark Ellison, Bill Foster, Drew Grace, John and Tom Leeson, Tony Pontifex, Mike Wade, Ian Young, Paul Byfield, Nigel Bewsher, Nick and Gordon Brooks, James Hunter, Dave Carton, The Austridge Family, The Desborough Family, Sue and Steve Cluney, The Lawries, Ian Firla, Tim Soutar, The Griffins, Con Griffin, Ian Mackley, Roger Counter, Rob Hadgraft, Chris Pike, John Clarke, Bernard Wilson, David Johnson, Big John Fenwick and Linda, The Braughtons, Zoe and Andy Kingsmell, All Farts - ancient and modern, The Baters, Ken Daniel, Richard Coe, All the Blackheath Walkers, Luca Ercolani, Rob Brown, Terri Shotton, John and Margaret Baldwin, Steve Hollingdale, Norman Dale, Barry O'Gorman, David Holden, Dan Lawson, Leon Bustin, Ted Sampson, George Murray, Brian Saxton, Wilf Orton, Mike Davies, The Algers, Stan Ridgewell, Carla Ferrari, The Pairmans, The Evendens, Adrian Stocks, Adrian MacDermott, Shankara Smith, All at Sri Chinmoy Marathon Club, Geoff Oliver, William Sichel, Barbara Terry, Tom Farrell, Alan Young, Wendy Edwards, Mike Martineau, Alan Morrison, Brian and Dave Shurmer, The Harrons, The Pearts, The Freemantles, The Nuttalls, The Bourtons, The Molnars, The Gassons, Steve Fletcher, Alan Stevens, Mark Gordon, Ray Gibson, Len Dalmon, Ian Cayzer, Colin and Shirley Poole, Ali Brand, Martyn Longstaff, All the Platts, All the staff at Norman Park Community Sports Centre, John Roberts, Mark Stafford, Brian Feldman, The Hubbards including John "Mr President", Bob Thomas, John Isaacs, Gareth Lloyd, Colin Rowe, Matt Bullen, John Julius Day, Harry Schmidt, Matt Maddocks, Glen Read, John Taylor, The Pickerings, Ian and Faye Scott, Gareth Evans, Paul Kerekgyarto, Will Brindley. Damian Hayes, Sheridan Morris, All the Vets Teams, Ray Walsh, Bob Cliff, Trevor and Erica, Helen Stephen and family, Kyara, Eva and Lennard, Iain and Jac, Bronwyn and Michael, Thomo and Heather, All Park Runners especially at Peckham Rye Park, Dartford Central Park and Foots Cray Meadow, all other Club members and anyone that I have left out!

Milton Keynes UK
Ingram Content Group UK Ltd.
UKHW052249160524
442738UK00004B/7